The Complete Pickett's Mill Battlefield Trail Guide

Brad Butkovich

Copyright © 2021 Historic Imagination LLC

www.historicimagination.com

All rights reserved.

ISBN-13: 978-1-7325976-3-1

Table of Contents

Introduction 3

The Battle of Pickett's Mill 5

Pickett's Mill Park Trail Map 13

The Blue Loop 15

The White Loop 35

The Red Loop 47

The Orange (Brand House) Loop 63

The Cabin 71

Order of Battle 73

Introduction

On May 27th, 1864 the Battle of Pickett's Mill was fought in Paulding County, Georgia as part of the Atlanta Campaign of the American Civil War. It was not a large battle by Civil War standards. However, it was intense, often fought at close range, and devolved into hand-to-hand combat at times. Several of the men who fought there considered it the most brutal and harrowing experience they endured during the war.

The war ended. Life continued for the soldiers and communities in rural Georgia. Modern growth was held at bay for decades in this rustic part of the state, but eventually progress made itself known. Housing developments and shopping malls gradually replaced pasture and farmland. Despite this, time has been kind to the land on which the battle was fought. By the 1950s the core of the battlefield was owned by a timber company, who used the land for its lumber resources. Eventually, by the 1970s more historic-minded individuals purchased the land, and then sold it to the state for preservation. The core of the battle field would be saved from further development. More than 700 acres would be preserved, and the park opened to the public in 1992. An oasis in the suburbs, the park can be enjoyed by both history and nature lovers alike. Whether it's touring the ridges and ravines to study the battle, or enjoying the pristine landscape for its beauty and wildlife, the park has something to offer for everyone.

The Complete Pickett's Mill Battlefield Trail Guide is meant to provide a comprehensive tour of the Pickett's Mill Battlefield State Historic Site for the casual visitor and hiker. There are four main walking trails in the park, and each one has tour stops highlighting the action that took place at that location during the battle, or interesting facts about the landscape itself. This book expands upon the park literature to offer a more detailed account of what happened, while not getting bogged down by the minutia of a full-scale history. Also included are several "extra" waypoints along the trails. These provide more historical details, often first person accounts delivering a powerful "this happened right here" experience.

The book has two main sections. The first is a brief overview of the battle with a series of maps to help the reader understand what happened during that late afternoon in 1864. This can be particularly useful for descendants of participants who wish to understand their ancestor's role in the battle, and follow in their footsteps as closely as the park trails allow. The second, main body of the book contains a detailed description of what happened at each marker along the trails, with pictures to help aid in visualization and orientation. By the very nature of the book, some back and forth flipping between the battle maps and trail maps is inevitable. Trying to include every stage of the battle superimposed upon the trail maps and markers would be a mess. However, the text includes page references to specific maps to make things easier for the reader. Some of the pictures were also taken in the winter. While the battle was fought in May, many landscape views are better seen during the cooler months where foliage does not obscure the view. Terrain is a critical part of Pickett's Mill, and being able to view and understand it is the key to the battle. A brief order of battle finishes out the book.

Pickett's Mill Creek was often called Pumpkinvine Creek or Little Pumpkinvine Creek by the participants at the time of the battle. The stream in the park is a tributary of Little Pumpkinvine Creek, which flows into Pumpkinvine Creek north of Dallas. The modern name is used. Also, quotes are left as-is with all misspellings in place.

For a more in-depth description and analysis of the battle, read *The Battle of Pickett's Mill: Along the Dead Line* also by this author. It is available at the Pickett's Mill Visitor's Center as well as many common online stores and venues. Enjoy your hike!

I wish to thank my children Anya, Lexi, and Jack for wanting to come out in the woods with me and hike the trails as I double-checked everything and took pictures. I also wish to thank Scott Felsen, Dillan Lee, and Ed Best for looking over the manuscript and giving me feedback. Thank you everyone!

The Battle of Pickett's Mill

May 27th, 1864 dawned on the Union and Confederate armies arrayed in Paulding County during the fourth week of the Atlanta Campaign of the American Civil War. Since May 5th, three Union armies commanded by Major General William T. Sherman had been marching south, generally along the Western & Atlantic railroad connecting Chattanooga and Atlanta. The Confederate Army of Tennessee under General Joseph E. Johnston opposed them. Several times the two forces met in battle, notably Rocky Face Ridge, Resaca, and Cassville, with smaller skirmishes in between almost every day. By May 20th, Johnston was forced to retreat south of the Etowah River and took up a strong defensive position along the railroad near Allatoona Pass.

After a few days of rest, Sherman resumed his advance. Instead of crossing the Etowah and confronting Johnston's formidable defenses directly, he decided to move around and behind the Confederates. Crossing the river near modern day Euharlee, Sherman's objective was the small rural town of Dallas. Once his three armies converged on the town, they would turn east and strike the railroad at Marietta. This would put Sherman's armies between Johnston and his supply base at Atlanta, trapping the Confederate army. The Union armies began moving on May 23rd.

Things did not go according to plan. Johnston discovered the move immediately, and intercepted Sherman's men at the New Hope Church crossroads on May 25th. Fighting from behind earthen trenches, the Confederates stopped the Northern advance. Sherman spent May 26th deploying his armies left and right trying to find the end of the Confederate line and attack their flank instead of head-on. On the morning of May 27th, Sherman came up with a bolder plan. Two divisions, about 14,000 men, would swing wide to their left (east) and try to get into the rear of the Confederates. Or at best, find the end of the Confederate trenches and attack their flank. The two divisions would come from the Army of the Cumberland and be led by Major General Oliver O. Howard.

Moving 14,000 men through the woods is no easy task, and the movement was quickly discovered. Earlier in the morning a Confederate brigade under Brigadier General Daniel C. Govan had moved to the modern day intersection of Mount Tabor Church Road and the Dallas Acworth Highway on a reconnaissance mission. After a sharp skirmish, he encountered Howard's large force moving east and southeast. Falling back to the main Confederate line, Govan and southern cavalry kept their commanders informed of the movement.

Govan's commanding officer was Major General Patrick R. Cleburne, and his division of 5,000 men held the end of the Confederate line. Hailed as the best division commander in the Army of Tennessee, his men were allowed to keep their distinctive blue battle flags as a testament to their courage following the army reorganization in the winter. Now they had the daunting task of holding the flank for the entire army.

Howard's men continued their march southeast. At points, they would turn south to find out if they had passed the Confederate flank, only to discover southern earthworks confronting them. Turning east, they continued marching and tried again. Eventually they made their way to a large wheat field and the end of Cleburne's earthworks. Howard had found the flank. He hadn't gained the rear of the Confederate army, but the day was drawing to a close. It takes time to form that many men into formations suitable for an attack. The end of the line would have to suffice.

Once everyone was ready, Howard gave the order to attack. Unfortunately, he and the lead division commander, Brigadier General Thomas J. Wood, choose to send his units in one at a time, instead of sending all 14,000 men in at once. A recipe for disaster was in the making, and Cleburne was ready for them.

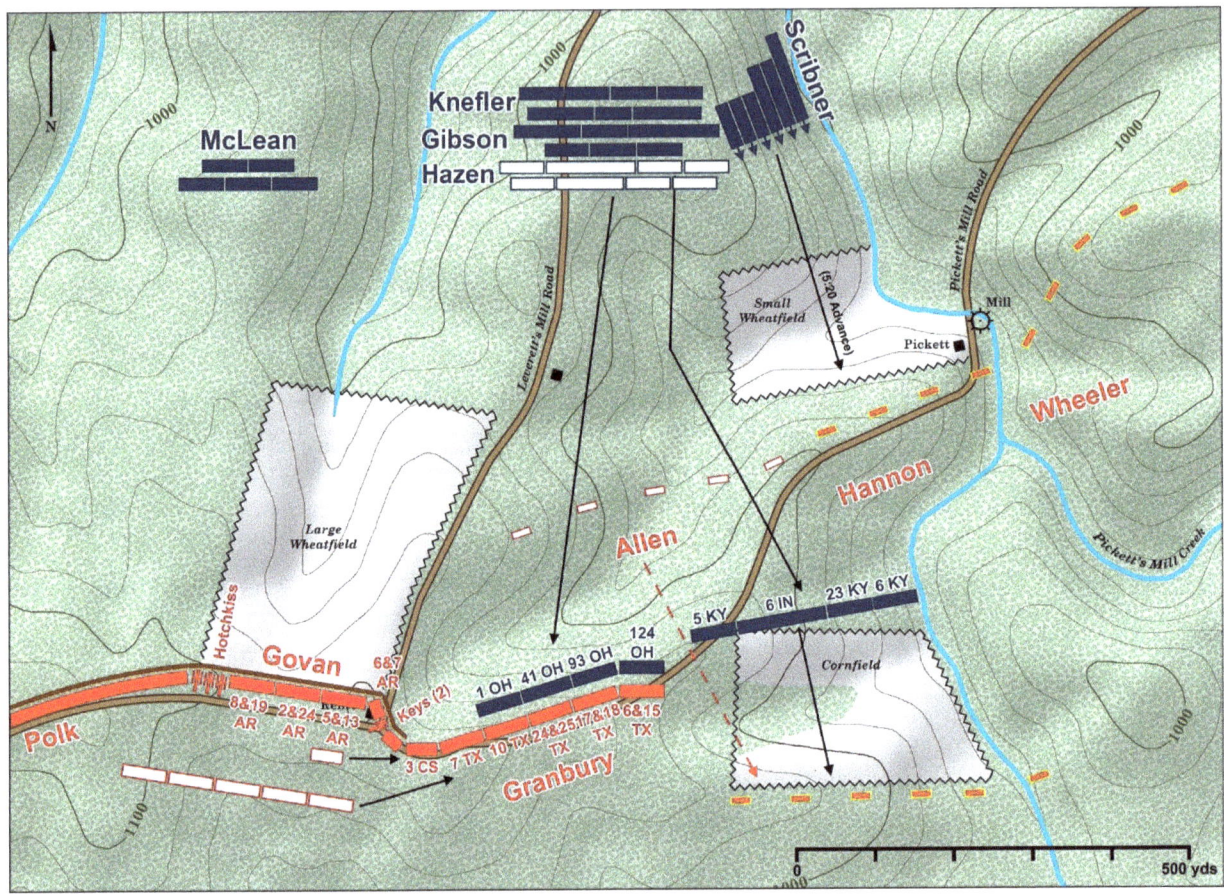

General Cleburne was aware of the Union force preparing to attack, but at the time, his line ended at the intersection of the Pickett's Mill and Leverett's Mill roads. There, a section of two 12 lb. howitzers from Key's Arkansas Battery guarded the flank of the army. Cleburne ordered General Hiram B. Granbury to take his brigade from behind Govan's position and extend the line further along the ridge. The Texans ran down the road, turned left and entered the woods a few yards for a better view into the ravine below. They were there less than 10-15 minutes before the Federals arrived.

The attack began just before 5 o'clock. Brigadier General William B. Hazen's brigade of eight regiments was in the standard Union formation of two lines; four in front and four in back. They surged forward and pushed back the Confederate cavalry skirmishers opposing them, but the organized formations soon broke down in the thick woods. As the brigade neared the bottom of the ravine, the first line began to drift to the right, and the second line to the left.

The first line of Ohio regiments descended into the ravine, reorganized, and marched to the top. There Granbury's men were waiting for them. As they gained the military crest, the Texans opened fire at a range of only 10-20 yards, stopping them cold. Both sides lay down or found cover behind trees and rocks, and a raging firefight began. Meanwhile, Hazen's second line moved past the end of the Confederate infantry to an old, open cornfield. By accident, Hazen was in a perfect position to turn the flank of the Confederate army and win the battle.

Support was on the way, but it was delayed. Colonel Benjamin F. Scribner's brigade was supposed to guard Hazen's left and prevent any surprises, but he did not advance until sometime after 5 o'clock.

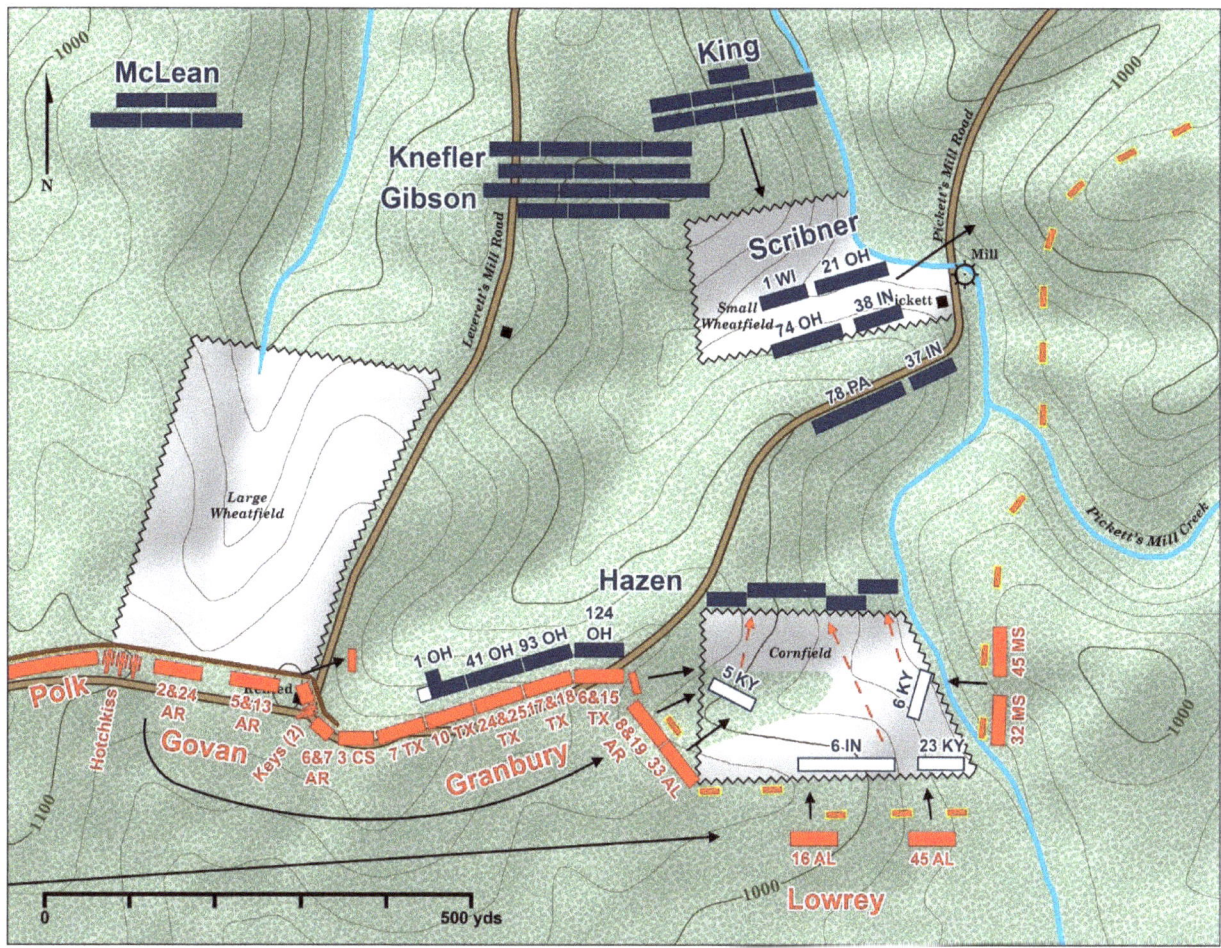

Hazen's first line and Granbury's Brigade continued to battle it out at the ravine. Key's Battery fired into their flank and beyond. Some rounds even traveling as far as Scribner's brigade near the creek. Govan sent skirmishers forward to fire into the Ohioan's flank, causing the 1st Ohio to refuse its line.

Hazen's second line reorganized at the northern end of the cornfield, and continued their advance. The 6th Indiana and 23rd Kentucky reached the opposite fence, and a brutal firefight erupted between them and the rebel cavalry attempting to stall them.

Help was on the way for the Confederate horsemen. Granbury could see the Federals moving past his open right flank, and he informed Cleburne. The division commander ordered Govan to send help, and committed another brigade as well. Govan sent the 8th & 19th Arkansas on the run, and they charged into the 5th Kentucky. Brigadier General Mark P. Lowrey's Brigade was not far behind. While the cavalry slowed the enemy's advance, Lowrey ran his men to the cornfield and beyond. Once in position, they charged and attacked from three sides. Hazen's second line was forced to retreat back to the cornfield's northern fence. There they rallied and brought the pursuing Confederates to a halt. Lowrey's men retreated to the cornfield's southern fence, and the two sides began exchanging fire across the field.

Where was Scribner? He was supposed to prevent this exact thing from happening. As soon as his brigade reached the top of the ridge at the Pickett house they stopped. Rifle fire from the Confederate cavalry across the creek began hitting their flank and rear. The colonel of the 37th Indiana was wounded and Scribner halted.

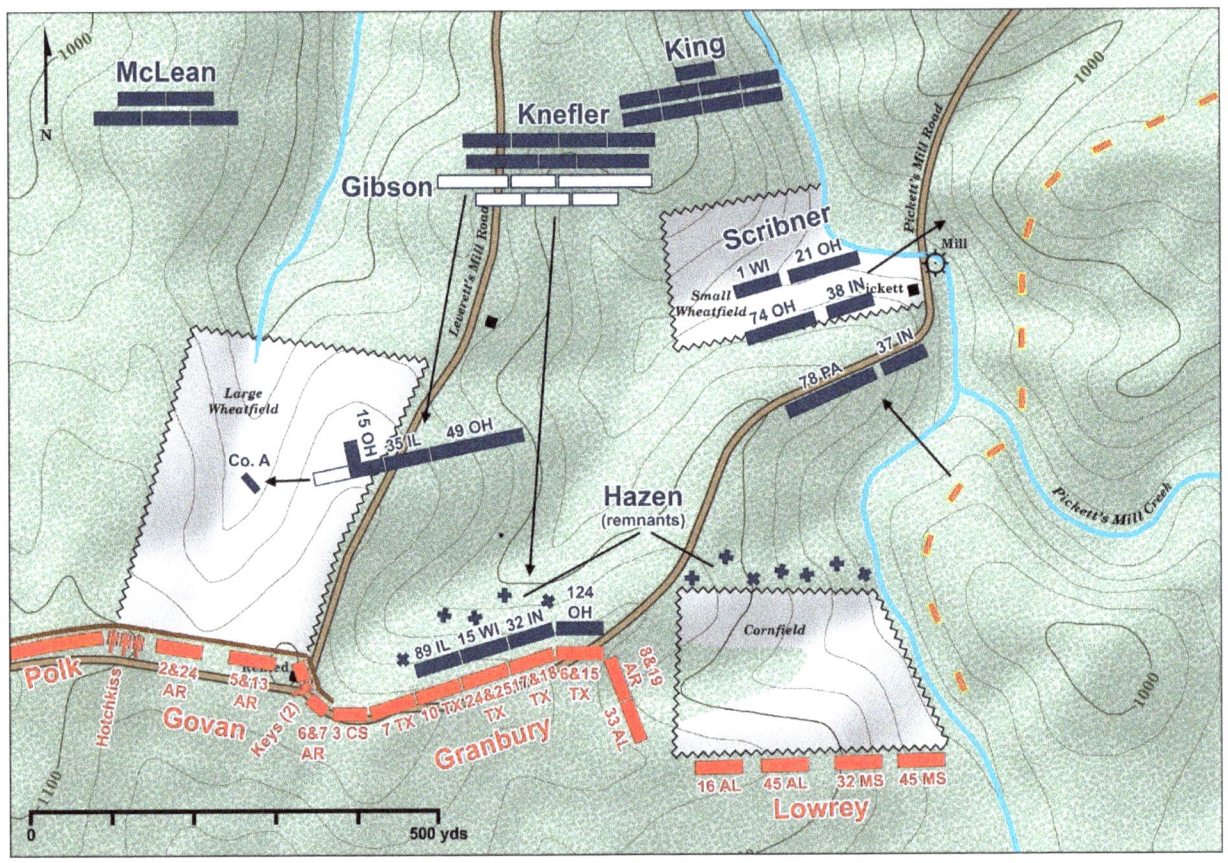

Hazen's attack stalled. The point blank fire in the ravine continued and the casualties on both sides mounted. From location near the corner of the cornfield, Hazen send back numerous messengers asking for support, but receives no answer. He ordered his brigade to withdraw. Many successfully retired, but hundreds remained, including most of the 124th Ohio.

Unknown to Hazen, General Wood had ordered the next brigade to advance. Colonel William H. Gibson ordered his men forward. Gibson kept a better handle on his brigade, and they advanced in one direction. The first line went down and up the ravine, through Hazen's men, and received the same greeting from the Texans. They too found cover where they could and fired back.

Gibson temporarily held the second line in reserve. The 15th Ohio entered the large wheat field and immediately took fire from Govan's infantry and Major Thomas R. Hotchkiss' artillery battalion. Company A deployed as skirmishers, and then half the regiment pulled back.

Now that Hazen had been halted at the cornfield, the 78th Pennsylvania and 37th Indiana faced attacks by Confederate cavalry and some of Lowrey's infantry. According to the 78th's historian they, "did not have any very definite line of battle, but they seemed to be in countless numbers, and they did not waver until, at some points, in front of the 78th Regiment they were not ten paces from our line." They kept the pressure on Scribner's front, and the fire from across the creek continued. Scribner ordered three of his regiments to cross the creek and drive the Confederate cavalry from his flank.

Brigadier General Nathaniel C. McLean was supposed to move his brigade forward to the edge of the large wheat field. His mission was to distract the Confederates and protect Hazen, and Wood's, other flank. He completely failed in his mission, and at some point during the attack withdrew most of his brigade without orders.

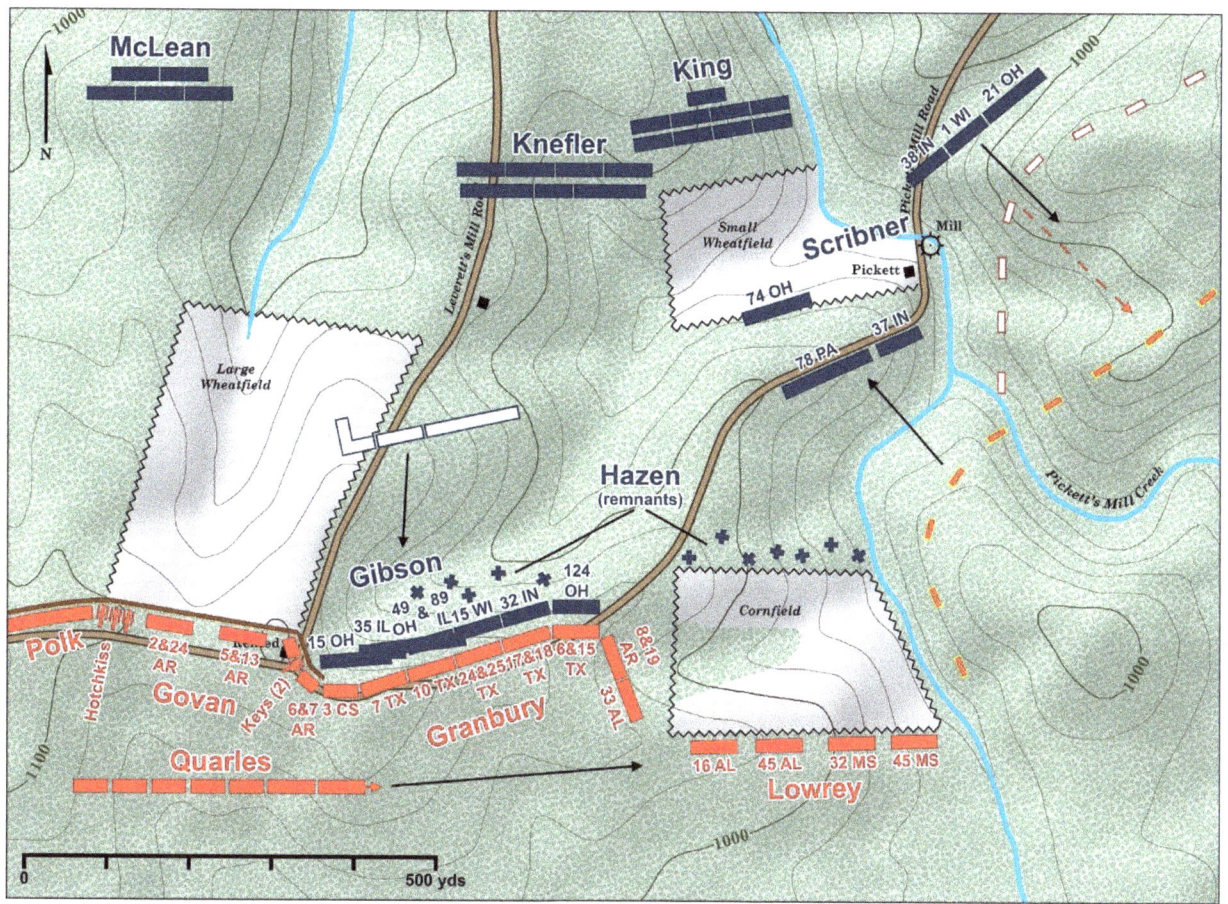

After momentarily holding them in reserve, Gibson ordered his second line forward. They too mixed with Hazen's men and their own forward line, but were brought to a halt just as savagely. The brigade fought severely intermingled. Some of the Confederates recalled the different lines as 3 or more waves. The sun was now setting, and it quickly began to get darker below the tree canopy because of prolonged gunfire and smoke.

Several survivors noted a curious aspect of the battle. There was a dead space between the two lines that no living person could cross. Casualties were steady, of course, but any time a group of men organized a charge toward the Confederate lines all guns were brought to bear upon them. Few survived. As recalled by future author Ambrose Bierce,

> The fire is, of course, as deadly at twenty paces as at fifteen; at fifteen as at ten. Nevertheless, there is the "dead-line," with its well-defined edge of corpses—those of the bravest. Where both lines are fighting without cover—as in a charge met by a counter-charge—each has its "dead-line," and between the two is a clear space—neutral ground, devoid of dead, for the living cannot reach it to fall there.

The Confederate cavalry continued their attack on Scribner's front. However, across the creek, the three regiments sent by Scribner formed and launched their attack, driving the cavalrymen from the heights and securing the brigade's flank.

Reinforcements began to arrive for the Confederates. When the attack began, General Cleburne sent word up the chain of command for help. It began to arrive. The first unit to arrive was Brigadier General William A. Quarles' Brigade. They had only joined the Army of Tennessee that morning, fresh from Mobile, Alabama. They raced for the cornfield to help Lowrey.

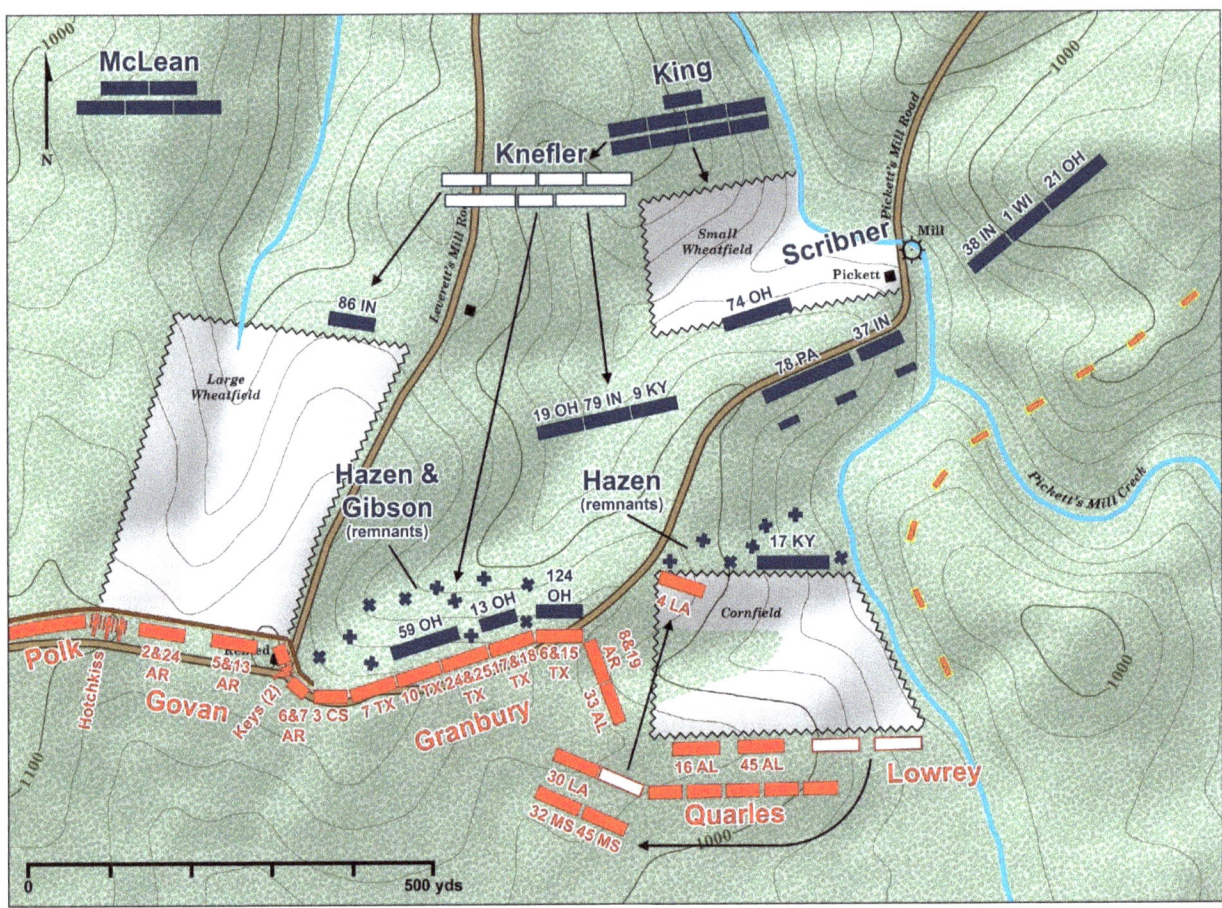

It continued to get darker. Wood decided to send in his final brigade commanded by Colonel Frederick Knefler. However, instead of another assault, they would provide covering fire so that the remains of Gibson and Hazen's commands could withdraw and bring their wounded with them.

Quarles Brigade arrived and took up a supporting position behind Lowrey. A gap existed between two regiments in Lowrey's Brigade, and Colonel Samuel E. Hunter ordered his 4th Louisiana forward to plug the gap. Instead of stopping in the gap, Hunter ordered a charge of the Union line across the cornfield. They reach the fence at the top of the hill and a vicious hand-to-hand struggle began, pushing the Federals back from that section of the fence.

Help was on the way. Two regiments of Knefler's front line entered the ravine and helped steady Hazen and Gibson's men. They began withdrawing the wounded. In small groups, men began to fall back. The 17th Kentucky drifted farther to the left, and ended up along the cornfield fence. They added their firepower to the fight against Lowrey, but began taking fire from the cavalry across the small stream on their left.

Knefler's second line followed the 17th, and the renewed fighting at the cornfield drew them to the left. Knefler ordered the 86th Indiana on the right to move forward to the edge of the large wheat field. He essentially fulfilled the job McLean's brigade was supposed to, but did not have enough men to put up as large of a distraction.

Scribner stabilized his line now that his flank across the creek was secure. He continued to fight the Confederate horsemen across the stream to their south.

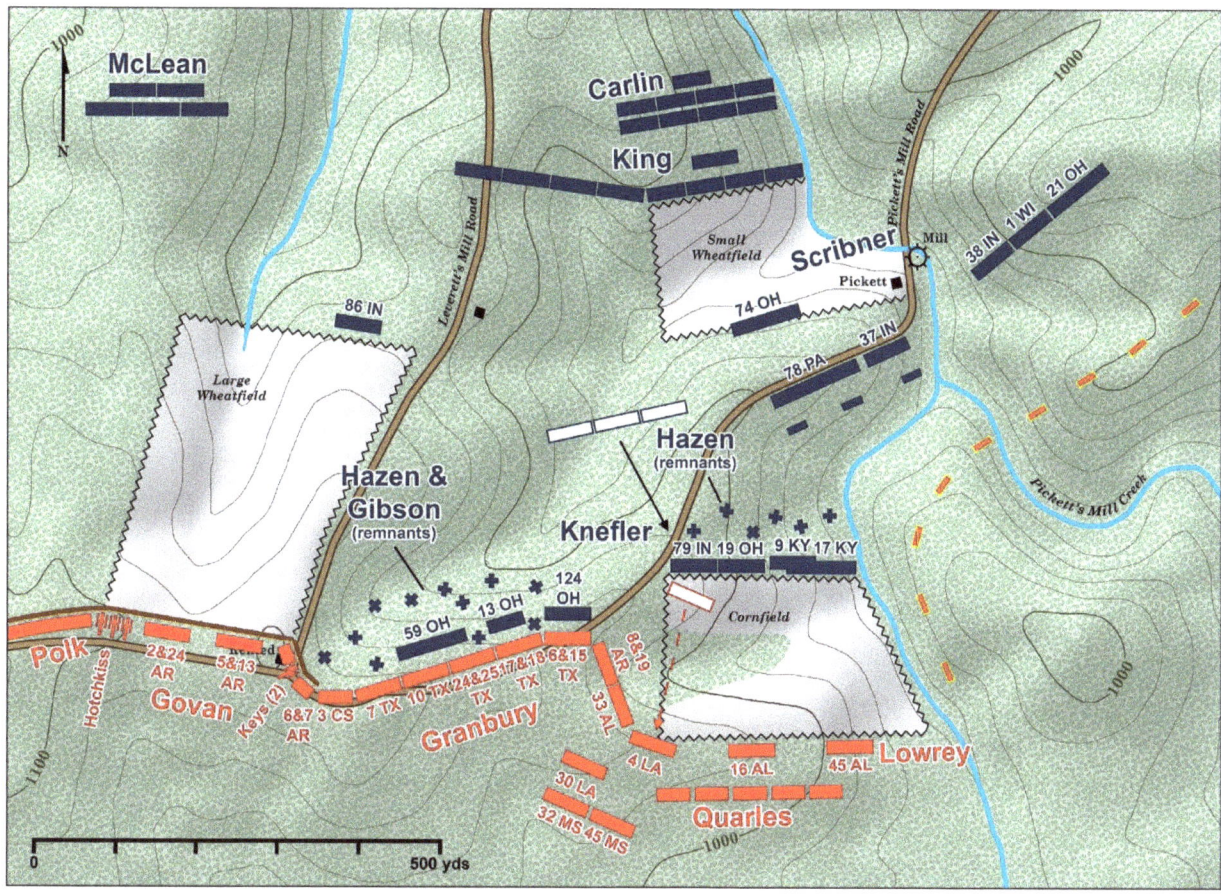

The Federal troops continued to withdraw their wounded under the cover of Knefler's men and any able-bodied soldiers that remained behind. It continued to rapidly get dark.

Knefler's second line moved south to the edge of the cornfield, and their numbers forced the 4th Louisiana to withdraw. It took its place in the gap in Lowrey's line. The 79th Indiana and 19th Ohio collected fence rails and logs and moved forward into the cornfield to the military crest. There they dropped the cargo and built a temporary barricade, using that cover to fire at the Confederates across the field.

The 9th Kentucky intermingled with the 17th Kentucky, and both continued to receive fire from across the stream to their left. Colonel Alexander M. Stout of the 17th Kentucky went back to confer with Colonel William Sirwell of the 78th Pennsylvania and asked him to advance his skirmishers so that they lined up with his regiment and protect his flank. Sirwell refused. Stout went directly to Colonel Scribner and asked him to order Sirwell to advance. Scribner refused as well. Knefler and Stout were left with the Confederates on their flank.

General Granbury was becoming anxious about his situation. The Union line was only yards away. They could hear the enemy moving through the underbrush. If they remained in position, a larger force could collect there during the night. Dawn could bring a charge from an entire Union division with little warning. A charge of 5,000 screaming soldiers from only 20 yards away leaves very little time to react. Granbury sent word back to Cleburne that he wished to charge and clear his front of the enemy. General Govan also sent couriers with the same message. The anxiety continued to build.

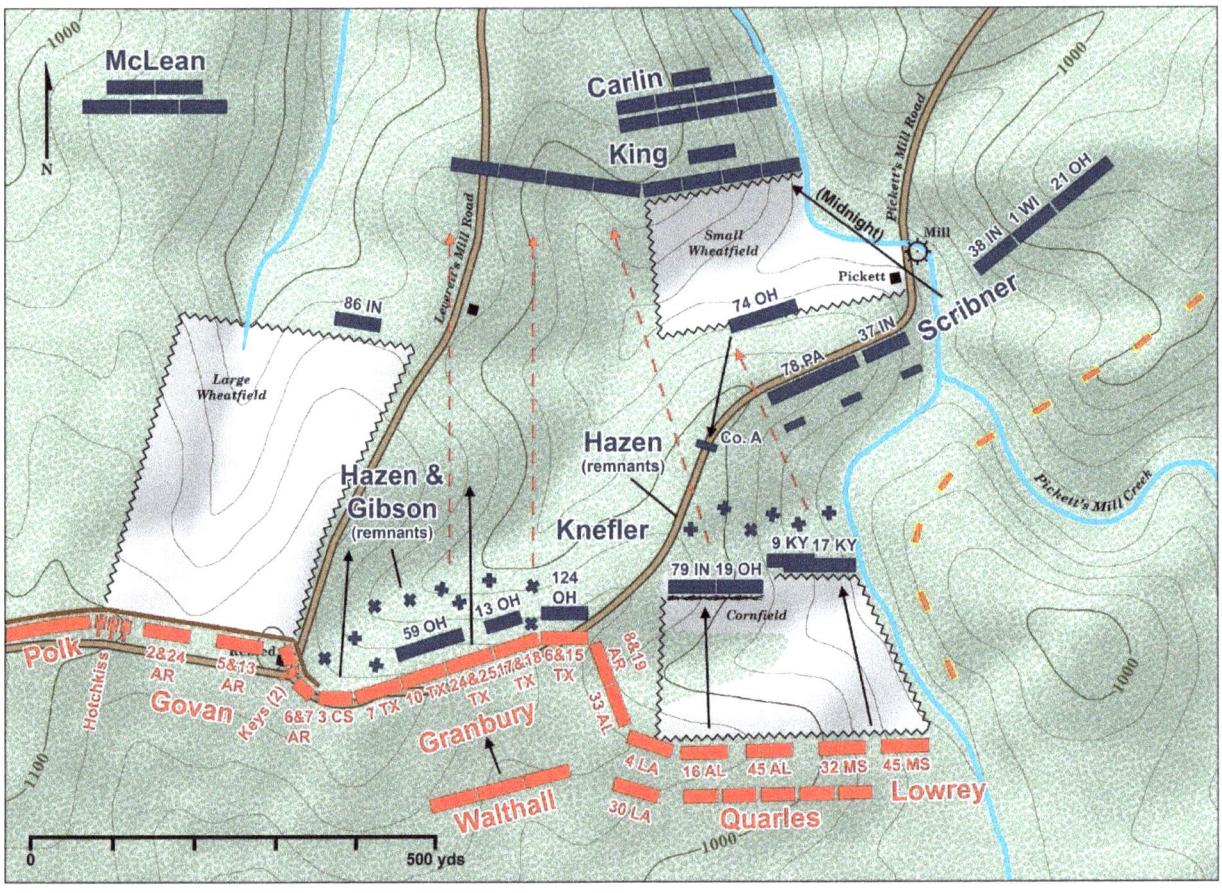

It was now dark. General Cleburne had been receiving request from his brigade commanders for permission to advance and push the enemy farther back from his lines. The front was relatively quiet, but gunfire still filled the air in burst. In the cornfield, both sides fired at the muzzle flashes at the opposite ends of the field. The large wheat field was quiet, thanks to McLean's failure to advance and occupy Govan's attention. More reinforcements arrived. Brigadier General Edward C. Walthall and his brigade marched up and took position behind Granbury. All the pieces were in place. With his flanks secure and support close at hand, Cleburne gave orders to his brigade commanders. The division would charge and drive away the enemy.

After some preparation, the bugles sounded the charge. Granbury and Lowrey's brigades leapt forward. In the ravine, the Federals fired a ragged volley and fled as fast as they could. The two sides intermingled at the bottom of the ravine and confusion reigned. Those wounded who could not be or had not yet been moved were taken prisoner, as were the slow and unlucky. The Confederates charged up the other side of the ravine, and established a skirmish line on its opposing height.

At the cornfield, Knefler's brigade and the remaining Federals also withdrew. Suddenly, Scribner had to deal with another exposed flank. He ordered the 74th Ohio to send skirmishers to protect the line. Company A was sent to the right along the ridge. They ran into Lowrey's men, but neither side had a taste for further combat. Scribner stayed in his position until about midnight, then quietly withdrew behind Union lines. With his withdrawal, the Battle of Pickett's Mill came to an end.

Pickett's Mill Park Trail Map

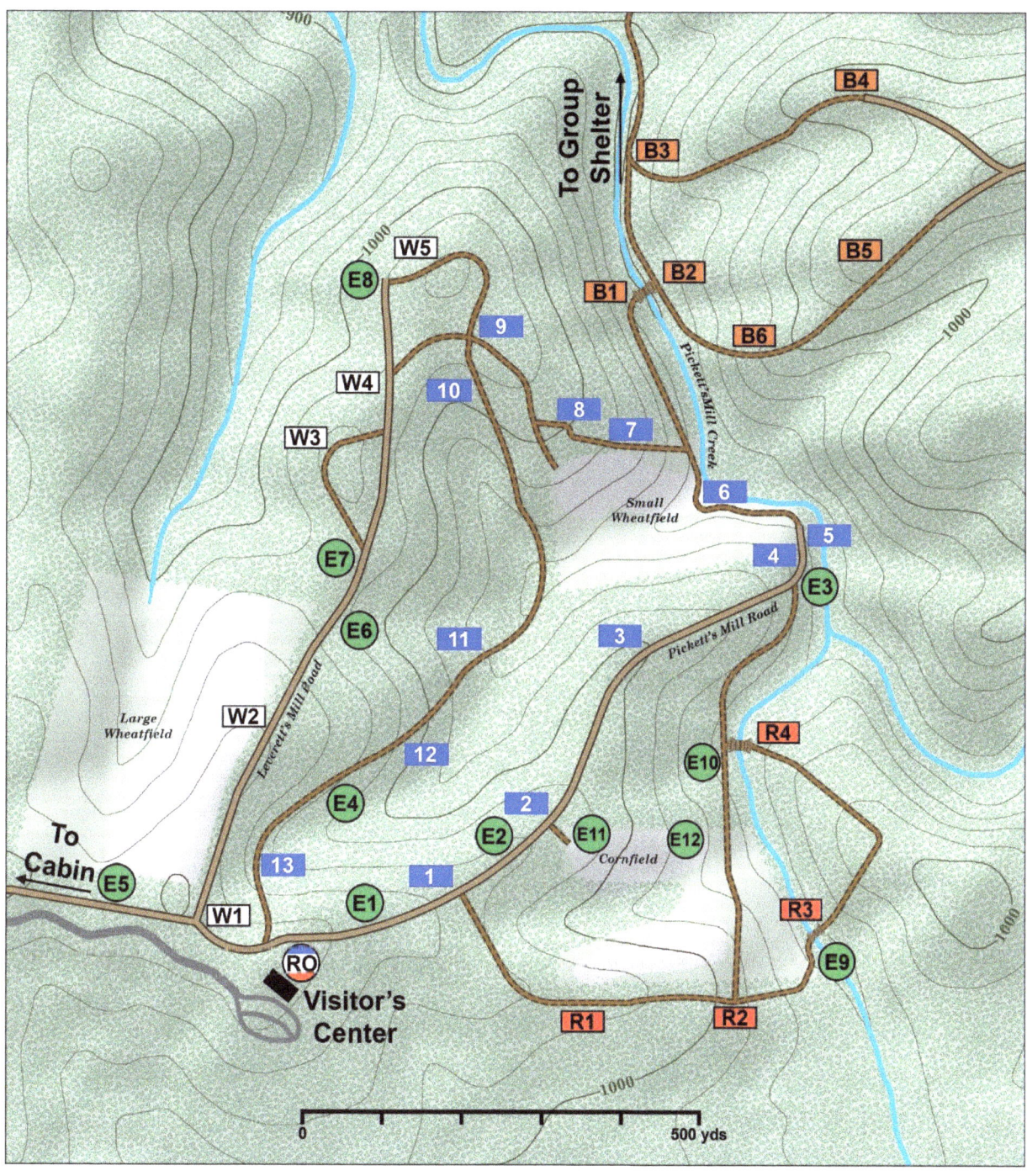

The Pickett's Mill Battlefield State Historic Site contains four main trails.

Blue Loop
- 1.5 miles.
- Most economical and informative if time is an issue.
- Blue Loop stations are simple numbers to avoid confusion between "Blue" and "Brand."

Red Loop
- Complete loop is 2 miles.
- Partial loop is 1.2 miles.
- Most comprehensive and complete single loop.

White Loop
- 1.1 miles.
- Focuses on fight in the ravine and its approach.

Orange Loop (Brand House Loop)
- Approximately 3 miles depending on using the White or Blue trails for access.
- Focuses on fighting that occurred in the park for the week after the May 27th battle.

Trail Stations

There are stations along each trail loop. Some of them have informative plaques with additional information. Each station is identified by a numbered post or marker. Stations and text are accurate as of March 2021. GPS coordinates are provided for each station.

............Face this direction when reading marker text.
So for this one, face the marker, then turn right and read the text............

............Station number.

............Trail color.

The "Extra" stations are not official park stops, but areas where historically significant or interesting events occurred. It will be handy to have a compass available to orient yourself. Most smart devices should already have a compass app available.

- Trails cover a variety of terrain, including steeps slopes. Please use caution.
- Remain on the trail at all times.
- Preserve our history. Do not walk on the surviving trenches or earthworks.
- Do not collect any historic artifacts, plant life, or animals.

The Blue Loop

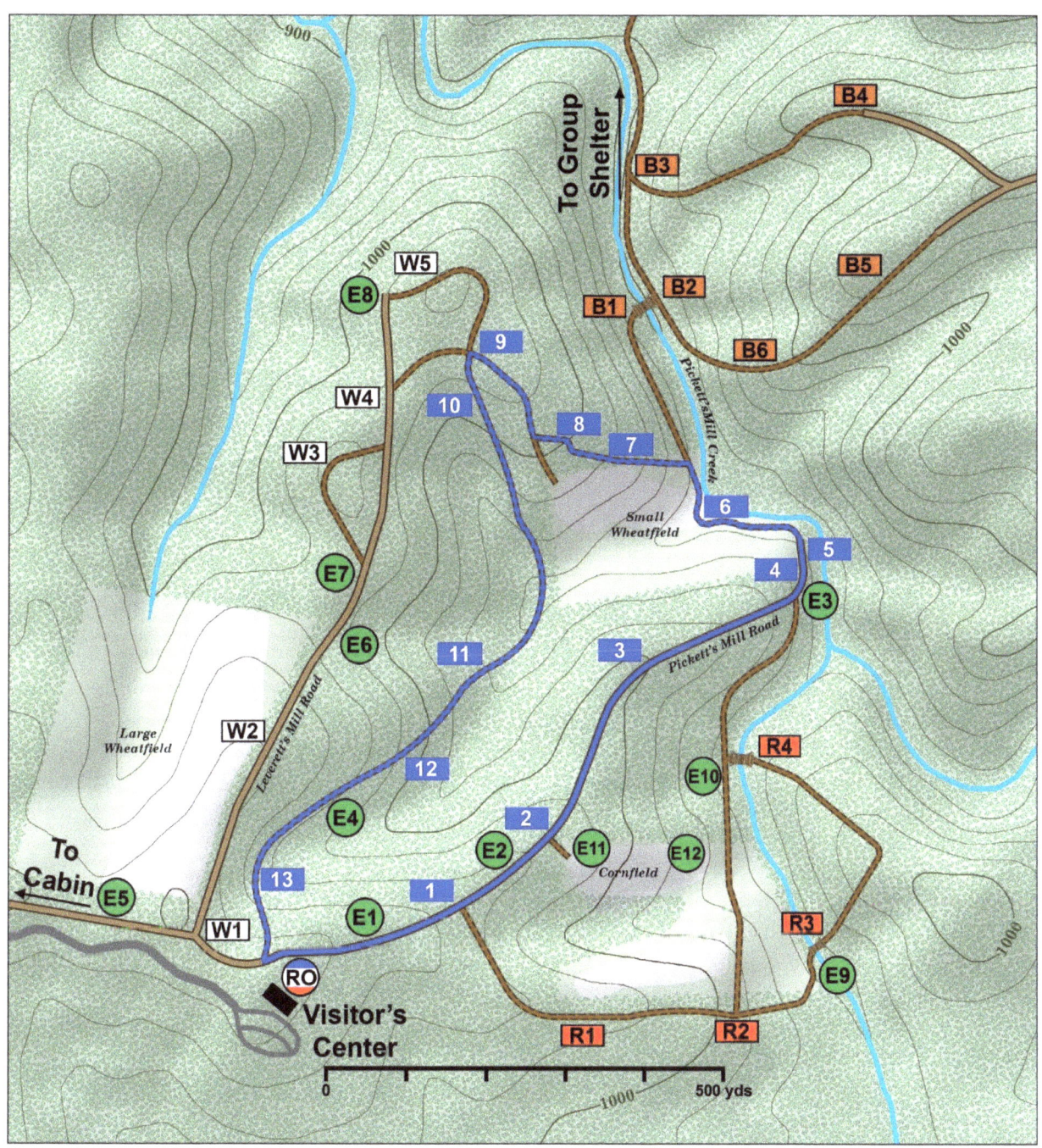

Ravine Overlook
33.9742, -84.7590

Stand on the elevated observation platform and look north. The wartime Pickett's Mill Road will be in front of you going left to right. You are standing at the left end of Granbury's Brigade. We don't know the exact order of each regiment in the brigade line, but this section was likely held by the 7th and 10th Texas regiments. Govan's Brigade would be to your left. Key's section of two 12 lb. howitzers would have been at the top of the hill to your left at the intersection of the Pickett's Mill and Leverett's Mill Roads.

Along this section and in this area, Major John R. Kennard of the 10th Texas walked along the line encouraging his men. "Put your trust in God, men. For He is with us." However, he couldn't resist taunting the enemy, and took up the cry "Come on—we are demoralized!" Almost immediately, a Union ball struck him in the head, and he fell. It was a serious but not life threatening wound. Raising himself up, Kennard exclaimed, "Boys, I told them a lie—and I believe that is the reason I got shot."

The Union approached this position from the opposite slope straight ahead. Colonel Gibson's brigade was heavily engaged with Granbury, Govan, and Key at this section of the line.

To walk the Blue or Red Loops, turn right and follow the road to the next stations. To hike the White Loop, turn left. Even if you do not plan on hiking the White Loop you might benefit from walking the short distance to station White #1 (page 37) just a short distance away and reading about Key's howitzers. Then return here to the Overlook and continue on another loop.

Extra #1
33.9746, -84.7585
Looking up toward the Confederate line from the Union perspective.
Taken off trail with park permission.

    If you stop at some point in-between the Ravine Overlook and the Blue #1 station, you will find yourself in the middle of Granbury's brigade line. Turn to the left and face north, then walk to the edge of the trail so that you can look into the woods. Granbury's line was only a few yards into the trees. You can make out only 20 or 30 yards away where the slope drops off sharply into the ravine. When the Hazen's Union line fully crested this precipice, the Texans opened fire at point blank range. Hundreds of men fell in the initial volley, then both sides took cover. This repeated when Gibson's brigade charged through Hazen's men during their attempt to dislodge the Confederates.

    William Oliphant of the 6th & 15th Texas Cavalry (dismounted) remembered a scene years later. During Gibson's attack, the 32nd Indiana charged this portion of the line, or perhaps a little to the right. The 32nd was largely recruited from Lawrenceburg, and Oliphant lived there as a young boy until his family moved to Texas. According to Oliphant,

> The color-bearer of the regiment fell with his colors, instantly another seized the flag and held it aloft only to fall dead. Again and again it was raised until six brave men yielded their lives in trying to keep it flying. The sixth man fell with the flag in front of our company only about ten or twelve feet from us… When the Indiana regiment broke and fell back leaving the flag on the ground at our feet one of the federals turned and seeing it was being left behind threw down his gun, came back and picked it up. He straightened himself to his full height, gritted his teeth and flapped his flag in our faces. Instantly a half dozen rifles were leveled on him…but just then one of our boys cried out, "don't shoot him, he's too brave." We lowered our rifles and gave him a cheer as he carried his flag safely away.

Oliphant would later learn that the flag was made by his aunt, who remained in Lawrenceburg.

Blue #1

33.9747, -84.7577

Granbury's line from the Confederate perspective.

You are near the right end of Granbury's brigade. The Pickett's Mill Road continues ahead. The Red Loop trail to your right was not present during the battle. Here the 6th & 15th Texas Cavalry (dismounted) anchored the end of the line. It stretched along the slope in to your left, and curved around in front of you across the road. It likely bent back and touched or crossed the road facing east. It primarily fought the 124th Ohio a short distance away.

From here, the Confederates could see Hazen's second line crossing the road farther downhill and getting into a position to flank them, or get behind the army. General Granbury sent messengers for help, and Govan sent the 8th & 19th Arkansas regiment. They arrived, formed to the right of the Texans (to your right and behind you), and led by their previous commander Brigadier John H. Kelly, charged into the 5th Kentucky at the cornfield. Several of the right companies of the 6th & 15th charged with them. Their efforts, along with the arrival of Lowrey's Brigade, saved the Confederate right.

Captain Sebron Sneed of the 6th & 15th later relayed an amusing anecdote to his wife in a letter,

> The right of our regiment also charged the flankers and they retreated. Our boys took a few prisoners in the charge. We were getting nearly out of ammunition, the men having fired 50 rounds each. I scared one Yankee awfully. I had a large butcher knife in my hand that I had been using to cut a cartridge Box from one of the wounded men in order to give his ammunition to the others. I had just finished when Sam Piper came to me with a prisoner he had captured. I ran to him with the knife reased to cut his cartridge box off. The poor devil thought I intended to kill him and threw up his hands with the most pitiful face. I could not restrain a laugh at his despairing countenance.

Extra #2

33.9750, -84.7567

Looking uphill from the 124th Ohio (Captain George Lewis) toward the 6th & 15th Texas Cavalry (dismounted).

Walk down the hill from station Blue #1 until just near the bottom. Face back up the hill. You are now near the end of Hazen's front line, at the left flank of the 124th Ohio. They fought the 6th & 15th Texas farther up the slope. Hazen's second line passed behind you on the way to the cornfield.

Captain George W. Lewis of Company B, 124th Ohio wrote,

> About four o'clock in the afternoon I went over to the left of the line to see how the battle was progressing in that quarter, and met Lieutenant Stedman where an old road comes winding down the hill…He said: "Captain, we can hold this position until reinforcements come up, can we not?" I replied, "I think so, but what we want is to carry this hill." I was facing up the hill, and he stood with his face toward me, and so near that I could have laid my hand on his shoulder. All at once a great stream of blood spouted from his left breast. He gave me one look, as much as to say "my time has come," and sank in my arms, dead. I moved his body out of the road, and folded his arms across his breast…There on that lone hillside was sacrificed one of the very few absolutely brave men I ever knew.

Later that evening he led three volunteers to recover Stedman's body. They had just arrived when, there rang out the silvery notes of a bugle, so clear and soft one might have mistaken it for some night bird's call. Ort [Sergeant Orson Vanderhoef] said, "Captain, what's that?" I said, "I guess that is some artillery call. It is certainly not an infantry call." Ort. Said, "By God, it's the rebel forward, I've heard it many a time on picket, and we'd better be getting out of here pretty God damned quick." Just at this instant a rebel skirmisher stepped into the old road, and the blaze of his musket went away past where we stood. I whispered to separate instantly, and away we went down the hill.

Blue #2
33.9753, -84.7561
Union approach toward the Cornfield along the Pickett's Mill Road.

    From this station, Hazen's second line surged out of the woods to your left after pushing back the cavalry skirmishers trying to slow them down. Crossing the road you are standing in, the Federals reached the northern edge of the cornfield to your right and continued beyond. The attack at the cornfield offered the best chance of success during the battle. General Hazen established his headquarters near a tree across the road to your right. From there, he commanded his brigade and tried to coordinate the two wings.

    Colonel Knefler's second line also exited the ravine here and crossed the road on the way to the cornfield. If you wish, take the small trail behind you to see the northern end of the cornfield. You can visit stations Extra #11 (page 61) and #12 (page 62), and return to this spot to continue along the Blue Loop.

    As you walk along Pickett's Mill Road to station Blue #3 you will pass through the area held by Company A of the 74th Ohio as they protected the right flank of Scribner's brigade during the night.

Blue #3
33.9773, -84.7542
Confederate rifle pit.

    This section of the ridge was held by the Confederate cavalry as they attempted to slow down the Union advance. The cavalrymen were posted in a skirmish line. This was a loose formation with the men spaced several yards apart. On the offensive, a skirmish line was used to gain information on the enemy and report it back up the chain of command, giving the generals a better idea of what was going on. On the defensive they kept the enemy away from the main line, and prevented enemy skirmishers from gaining any information. During an attack, they served as an early warning system for those behind them so they weren't taken by surprise, and did their best to slow down the enemy advance.

    This last role is what the Confederate cavalry attempted to do against the oncoming Union infantry during the battle on May 27th. They were stationed along the ridge to your left, stretching in front of and behind you as far as you can see. Scribner's brigade pushed them back in this area, and Hazen's men forced them to retreat behind you.

    The shallow depression to your immediate left is a rifle pit, used for protection against enemy fire. There is a line of them along the north side of the road. Today it would be called a foxhole. There is a strong likelihood this rifle pit and others along the ridge were built and manned by Confederate infantry the week after the battle. The Confederate cavalry did not have time to dig them on May 27th. The infantry skirmishers here kept watch on King's brigade to the north. You can see the opposite end of the small wheat field during the winter. Confederate rifle fire from these skirmishers caused many casualties in the Union ranks across the ravine.

    In front of you to your right was the approximate location of the right flank of the 78th Pennsylvania as they fought on this ridge during the May 27th battle.

Extra #3

33.9777, -84.7530
Looking north from Scribner's position toward the attacking Confederate cavalry.
Taken off the trail with park permission.

    Position yourself at the intersection of the Blue and Red Loops. Look south with the Red Loop in front of you.

    When Scribner's brigade advanced it passed the Pickett farm and field behind you, ascended the ridge, and took position here. You are at the left flank of the 37th Indiana. The 78th Pennsylvania was farther down the ridge to your right. Both regiments were south of the road in the woods along the crest. Many of the soldiers in these two regiments picked up and carried logs and fence rails as they advanced. This was not the mindset of an aggressive force bent on charging the enemy. When the two regiments reached this position they dropped their cargo and used it for cover. In this position the two regiments fought for several hours against repeated attacks to your front by Confederate cavalry and infantry.

    Look to your left. When Scribner first arrived Confederate cavalry along the heights across the creek put a heavy fire into the left flank of the 37th Indiana. Because of this, Colonel Scribner decided to send half of his brigade across the creek to push the cavalrymen back and secure his position. This decision, coupled with the Confederate attacks up the slope in front of you, delayed any attempt to advance and help Hazen's men in the cornfield about 150 yards to your right front. This delay doomed the Union fight at the cornfield to defeat, and their best chance to win the battle.

    John J. Kirk of the 37th picked up a rotten log during the advance. A friend mocked him, but Kirk predicted, "You will be glad to get your head behind this log before long." Sure enough, as soon as the firing started his companion was beside him. "You made fun of me for carrying this chunk, and just as I said, you were the first man to get behind it."

Blue #4
33.9782, -84.7528
The Pickett House well.

The Pickett House stood at this location. It was the home of the widow Martha C. Fannin Pickett. Her husband, Benjamin W. Pickett had been killed at the Battle of Chickamauga on September 19th, 1863 while serving with the 1st Georgia Cavalry. The house and nearby mill were destroyed during the May 27th battle or shortly afterwards.

The Pickett's owned much of the land around the battlefield. In addition to the house and mill, they rented a cabin to an unknown family on the western edge of their property. This house is located at the intersection of the Pickett's Mill and Leverett's Mill Roads near station Extra #5 (page 38).

The well in front of you was dug by hand, and then lined with stones.

Blue #5
33.9788, -84.7528
Pickett's Mill dam foundation.

    The mill owned by the Picketts stood here. Facing to the left, as indicated by the arrow on the station post, you would be looking at the mill building downstream. The mill dam was to your right and the pond would be upstream and behind you. If you walk down to the creek to your right you can see part of the foundation for the mill dam (pictured above). The mill was used for food production. It ground corn and flour for the local community. The mill, along with the house, was destroyed during the battle or in the days shortly afterwards.

    Captain George W. Lewis of the 124th Ohio wandered near here as he made his way back to the Union lines after escaping the Confederate night attack (see Extra #2 on page 19). He would later write, "As soon as one was away from the light of the burning pines it was so dark one could not see a hand before him, and the first thing that I realized I was up to my neck in Picket's mill pond; but, being a Baptist, that did not astonish me to any alarming extent."

Blue #6
33.9788, -84.7540
Looking north across small wheat field toward Scribner's starting point.

You are looking east from the cleared farm land around the Pickett homestead. In 1864 this field was much larger. It extended farther to the west, behind you, a bit farther uphill to the left, and much farther to your right, going all the way to the Pickett house at station Blue #4.

Scribner's brigade formed for the attack on the edge of the field to your left front facing toward you, or south. The afternoon approach march had not been easy, and several casualties occurred before the main battle even started. Company A of the 78th Pennsylvania had their first man killed farther back in the woods as they approached this location. As they marched James Little was shot and fell. An officer raised him up as he lay dying, and Little told him, "Tell mother I am in the front ranks yet." He repeated the phrase three times and died in the arms of the regimental chaplain.

When Scribner's advance began, they moved toward you across this field. They were fired upon by the Confederate cavalry on the ridge to your right, as well as from across the creek in front of you. The larger Pickett's Mill Creek ahead of you, not the small stream to your left with the foot bridge. Scribner's rear units, the 1st Wisconsin, 21st Ohio, and 38th Indiana marked time in this field before being ordered across the creek to push back the Confederates there.

After Scribner advanced, Brigadier General John H. King's brigade of Regular Army infantry advanced and took their place. They soon began digging in and building earthworks to protect themselves.

Blue #7
33.9794, -84.7549
Looking uphill along the trenches of King's Regular Army brigade.

At this station to your right are earthworks begun by King's brigade as the battle was raging. During the next week they were continually enlarged and strengthened. King's brigade, and the brigade commanded by Brigadier General William P. Carlin behind them, were the only fresh troops available after the battle. They would have to defend against any Confederate counterattack. Fortunately for the Federals, the available Confederates were just as exhausted and no counterattack was launched against the Union main line that night.

The works behind you closest to the creek were actually out in the open field in 1864. They were manned by the 16th United States Infantry. During the day the men were essentially trapped in their trenches. To get up and expose yourself was asking for a bullet wound. The Confederates had a skirmish line on the ridge across the field to your left "The…day was a hot one," remembered Lieutenant Edgar R. Kellogg commanding Company F, "and the Confederates, a short rifle shot away, hidden by intrenchment's, trees and bushes, sent their bullets with deadly precision over the top of my parapet, making it impossible for my men to leave their trench for any purpose except at the risk of almost certain death or wound."

Unfortunately, this was graphically illustrated the same day, May 28th, when the regiment's commander ordered Kellogg to withdraw his company from the line in mid-day for service elsewhere. The sergeant relaying the order wisely yelled it to Kellogg form the tree line. Kellogg, his company's 1st Sergeant and ten men were the first group to run the gauntlet. "With this squad of leading men I ran from cover. In an instant half of these men were shot down." The regiment's commander mercifully rescinded the order and the rest of the company remained in place until dark.

Blue #8

33.9796, -84.7552

King's view along the small wheat field toward the Confederates on the far ridge.

From here, King's brigade of Regular Army soldiers kept watch over the small wheat field behind you and the Confederates beyond. To your right are more of the Union trenches. The men in them had to keep their heads down during the day. Any movement over the top of the trench would bring a hail of bullets, and often a painful or fatal wound. Major John R. Edie commanding the 15th United States Infantry wrote,

> The brigade remained in this position from the 27th of May till the 5th day of June, under fire all the time. Incessant vigilance and resolute determination were all these days necessary to hold the position. The enemy kept up during these days a continuous and fatal discharge of musketry, shell, and canister. The casualties at this point were numerous… The conduct of the officers and men during the nine days the command lay at this hazardous point is worth of great commendation, and I take great pleasure in bearing testimony to their gallantry.

19th United States' Lieutenant Arthur B. Carpenter wrote home,

> …our brigade has been in front all the time and has lost severely. our works are close to the rebel works, so that in some places no pickets or skirmishers are thrown out. we have to lay low or get picked off.

This position gives a good look at the different features of entrenched lines. Notice the trench to your right that is at a right angle to the ones facing the enemy. These provided covered access to the main line. They were also a fallback position in case the enemy breached the works farther down the earthworks. The occupants could pull back at right angles to the original trenches and still have earthworks to protect them and seal the breach.

Blue #9
33.9803, -84.7565
Assembly area for Wood's division.

Brigadier General Thomas J. Wood formed his division at this spot in the afternoon of May 27th. The trail you are standing in did not exist back then.

You are standing in the area the lead brigade under General Hazen assembled. It was in a formation with four regiments in front and four in a second line behind them. Behind them, likely stretching over the hill behind you, were the other two brigades in the division for a total of six lines of battle. Brigadier General Richard W. Johnson's division was likewise formed behind you and to your left. Approximately 14,000 men were gathered in this area waiting for the order to go forward.

The men in the ranks idled away the time in different ways. Lieutenant Ambrose Bierce, Hazen's topographical engineer and famous postwar author, went forward to study the enemy position. Some cooked their dinners. Others found time for a joke or two. The birds singing in the trees caused one soldier to remark that it would be a pity to frighten them, but by necessity there would be more or less noise soon. Others found time for a nap.

As the men waited, the commanders met to decide on strategy. Wood said to Howard, "We will put in Hazen and see what success he has." This startled Hazen, as it meant he would be attacking alone. General Howard concurred. "General," he said to Hazen, "you will have to charge and turn the enemy's flank if you sacrifice your brigade." With that, the decision was settled. Instead of 14,000 men attacking at once, less than 2,000 would be sent first. The rest of the division would follow, and there would be support on the flanks by McLean and Scribner. But Hazen would begin alone. This strategy contributed to the Union defeat during the battle.

Blue #10
33.9801, -84.7566

Trenches for King's brigade after the battle. Wood's division assembly area before the battle on May 27th.

The men of Wood's division formed here for the attack on May 27th. After they advanced, King's Regular Army brigade took over this position and began building earthworks. To your right is part of the trench system they built after the battle. Farming, erosion, and logging have taken their toll on them, and these faint remnants are all that exist. When Wood's men were repulsed, they fell back farther north of this position and regrouped, eventually moving to the hills to the northwest.

Despite being exhausted form the day's march, Wood's division began to dig in. War allow no rest. If the Confederates were to attack, either at night or in the early morning, survival depended on having earthworks built. The men did as best they could in the dark. It was not easy, and there was much confusion. In fact, when the men of the 124th Ohio woke up the next morning, the found they had built their works in the dark facing the wrong direction!

As you continue down the trail in front of you, imagine the scene of Hazen's initial advance on the 27th. It immediately became disorganized. By the time it reached this marker, the front line had drifted to your right, generally moving along the slope to your right as you walked down the trail. The brigade's second line drifted to the left, generally following the modern trail. As Ambrose Bierce later wrote,

> In less than one minute the trim battalions had become simply a swarm of men struggling through the undergrowth of the forest, pushing and crowding. The front was irregularly serrated, the strongest and bravest in advance, the others following in fan-like formations, variable and inconstant, ever defining themselves anew… The color-bearers kept well to the front with their flags, closely furled, aslant backward over their shoulders. Displayed, they would have been torn to rags by the boughs of the trees.

Blue #11
33.9768, -84.7567
View where Hazen's second line crested the ridge opposed only
by Confederate cavalry.

As Hazen's men moved forward, they were opposed by Confederate cavalry skirmishers from Brigadier General John H. Kelly's and Brigadier General William Y. C. Humes' cavalry divisions. They were no match for massed infantry, but they slowed them down as best they could. Posey Hamilton of the 10th Confederate cavalry described the initial encounter years later,

> The enemy approached in line, but had a picket line in their front… Lieutenant McKinnon stood near my side, on my left; Sergeant Ledbetter was the next man on my right. He caught sight of one of the enemy and fire, and at the crack of his gun, a man in our front cried out in the most pitiful, agonized tone that I ever heard; and he was so near that we thought he was one of our own men. Lieutenant McKinnon railed out: "Now you have played hell; you hot one of our own men." Ledbetter replied: "It was a Yankee." Lieutenant McKinnon's next order was: "Give them hell!"

From this marker, Hazen's second line advanced up the hill behind you and to your left. After crossing the Pickett's Mill Road along the crest, they continued south into the cornfield. Hazen's front line entered the ravine farther up to your left front, and began their assault from there.

Blue #12
33.9758, -84.7580
Union view of the ravine.

    You are now standing opposite the end of Granbury's line. At the top of the ridge to your left is Station Blue #1 (page 18). From about this spot the 124th Ohio charged across the ravine, up the hill, and confronted the 6th & 15th Texas Cavalry (dismounted). From left to right stretching in front of you, the 93rd, 41st, and 1st Ohio regiments advanced to the right of the 124th Ohio.

    Notice how steep the sides of the ravine are. This exhausted the soldiers moving forward, but it also provided shelter for the wounded. Exploding shells and solid shot from Key's two howitzers at the head of the ravine far in front of you caused many casualties. Even if they couldn't see the line directly, exploding shrapnel and falling limbs could still injure soldiers. Terrain played an important part in the battle.

    The Ohioans in this first line expected the second line to charge through them and drive the Confederates back. Colonel Oliver H. Payne of the 124th Ohio and Lieutenant Colonel Robert L. Kimberly of the 41st Ohio each sent multiple couriers to the rear to find the second line and bring them forward. Not all of the messengers made it alive, having to run down the ravine and then up the exposed slope to your right. But the second line was nowhere to be found. It had drifted to the left and was even then fighting in the cornfield.

    With no relief in sight and Hazen at the cornfield, the commanders of the front line took it upon themselves to order a retreat after 45 minutes to an hour after the fighting started. They made their way back in small groups. Most of the 124th Ohio remained on the line and in close combat. As the remnants of Hazen's brigade retired they met the soldiers of Gibson's brigade advancing, about thirty minutes too late.

Extra #4
33.9756, -84.7591
Looking across the Ravine toward Granbury's Brigade.

Face south, or looking down the slope and toward the other side of the ravine. You are opposite the right end of Hazen's first line, and roughly the middle of Gibson's line during their attack. If you look to your right, you can see the head of the ravine where Key's two howitzers had a direct line of sight to this area from station White #1 (page 37). They would have been able to fire canister at this range; deadly iron balls fired from the cannon like a shotgun.

Take a moment to consider the Union troops on the opposite slope. Notice all the rock outcroppings. Pick out a few individual boulders. Did a wounded soldier take cover behind that one? What drama played out at the bottom of the ravine that was never written down and is lost to history?

After the Union began their preparation to withdraw, covered by Knefler's brigade, General Cleburne launched his night attack. Their assault from close range caused panic and confusion. The Northerners fired a single volley and then fled into the darkness. Down they went into the ravine in front of you, and then back up the opposite side to this position and beyond. Everywhere was chaos and confusion. It was almost impossible to tell friend from foe. Charles A. Leuschner of the 6th & 15th Texas wrote,

> They would sometime be so mixt up that they could not tell wich was a Rebel or wich was the yankey's; and they would ask what regiment do you belong to, and sometimes the answer would be the 40th, and our boy's knew that we dit not have no 40th regt. in our brigade; and, therefore, they would Kill such. Sometimes the answer would be the 24th; and when they would ask the 24 What, 'the 24 Ohio,' and they were servt the same.

Blue #13
33.9752, -84.7594
Looking from Gibson's starting point toward the left of Granbury's line.

    From this station you are looking into the Confederate lines from the perspective of Gibson's Union brigade. The ravine is not as deep here, and the crossfire from Key's howitzers to your right front is much closer and more deadly. In front of you is the left end of Granbury's line, likely the 7th and 10th Texas. However, the right end of Govan's Brigade would also have been fighting here, namely the 3rd Confederate and 6th & 7th Arkansas regiments. Gibson's brigade advanced from this area until just a few yards away from the Confederate line near the Visitor's Center.

    Sergeant Major Andrew Gleason of the 15th Ohio wrote of the action near here,

> A galling cross-fire scorched the ravine and ridge alike, rendering it almost useless to seek shelter of tree or rock. I noticed two men taking shelter behind a medium sized tree, on the brink of the ravine, and when one of them was hit in the hand by a minnie ball and retired to the rear, I crept to his place behind the other. He was leaning against the tree and would not lie down, although he was not firing. In a few minutes a ball came from the left and struck him squarely in the temple, with that peculiar "spat," which once heard, is at once recognized as the passage of a bullet through flesh and bone. It killed him so suddenly that he never changed his position, and had I not heard the shot strike and been spattered by his blood and brains, I might have believed him still untouched. He was a stranger to me, evidently from another regiment, and being past all human aid, I soon left him, going to another tree where I could get a better view of the front.

    A staff officer to General Govan, Lieutenant John Litton Bostick, was with the 6th & 7th Arkansas to your right. From his location near Key's battery he could see down the Union line. He wrote,

> I fired at a Yankee on the right of the enemy's line not more than one hundred and twenty yards distant and had the pleasure of seeing him reel & fall… The first line of the enemy where they stood, almost in perfect line of battle. The brave Texans never yielded an inch before the overwhelming force opposed to them, but fired with all the steadiness and coolness that they could have exhibited if firing at game.

The White Loop

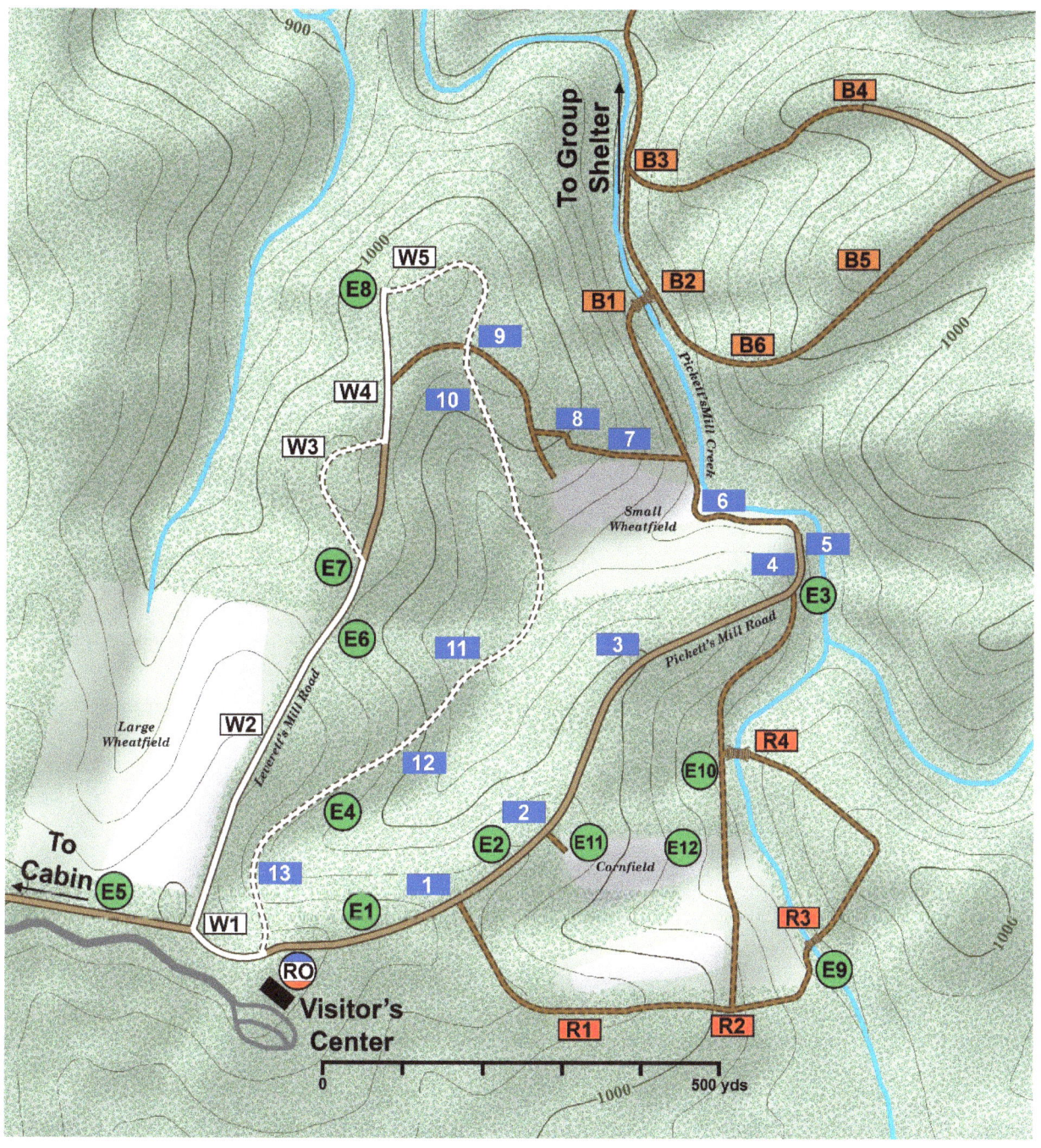

Ravine Overlook
33.9742, -84.7590

Stand on the elevated observation platform and look north. The wartime Pickett's Mill Road will be in front of you going left to right. You are standing at the left end of Granbury's Brigade. We don't know the exact order of each regiment in the brigade line, but this section was likely held by the 7th and 10th Texas regiments. Govan's Brigade would be to your left. Key's section of two 12 lb. howitzers would have been at the top of the hill to your left at the intersection of the Pickett's Mill and Leverett's Mill Roads.

Along this section and in this area, Major John R. Kennard of the 10th Texas walked along the line encouraging his men. "Put your trust in God, men. For He is with us." However, he couldn't resist taunting the enemy, and took up the cry "Come on—we are demoralized!" Almost immediately, a Union ball struck him in the head, and he fell. It was a serious but not life threatening wound. Raising himself up, Kennard exclaimed, "Boys, I told them a lie—and I believe that is the reason I got shot."

The Union approached this position from the opposite slope straight ahead. Colonel Gibson's brigade was heavily engaged with Granbury, Govan, and Key at this section of the line.

To walk the Blue or Red Loops, turn right and follow the road to the next stations. To hike the White Loop, turn left. Even if you do not plan on hiking the White Loop, you might benefit from walking the short distance to station White #1 (page 37) just a short distance away and reading about Key's howitzers. Then return here to the Overlook and continue on another loop.

White #1
33.9746, -84.7602
Looking from Key's position into the Union flank.

This intersection is one of the critical landmarks of the battle. The Pickett's Mill Road is to your left and right. It is the road you walked along from the Visitor's Center. The Leverett's Mill Road is to your front and continues north until it crosses Pickett's Mill Creek at its namesake mill and homestead.

When Howard arrived this was the right end of the entire Rebel army. Govan's Brigade ended here. Eying the terrain and seeing the line of fire the ravine to your right front provided, General Cleburne ordered the commander of his artillery battalion to station cannon to fire down its length. A two gun section of 12 lb. howitzers from Key's Arkansas Battery took position here. Their shot, shell, and canister inflicted numerous casualties among the Federals moving and fighting in the ravine.

There are conflicting accounts concerning the placement of Key's two gun section. Some participants say the cannon were at the very end of the line. Others say it was placed in the middle of the 6th & 7th Arkansas, the right-most regiment of Govan's Brigade. As Hazen's brigade approached, Cleburne sent Granbury's Brigade at the run along the Pickett's Mill Road to extend the line even further.

Lieutenant John Litton Bostick on Govan's staff later wrote to his sister about the effects of Key's battery firing from this location. He noted that the enemy,

> sought shelter behind trees, rocks or anything that could save them from the terrible storm in front. But the shelter, which shielded them from Granbury's fire, afforded them no protection from the deadly aim of the Arkansas brigade which poured a galling fire into their right flank. They gave up all idea of advancing on account of…Key, which swept with canister and shell, the ravine and exposed hillside to their rear, they sought safety in lying flat upon the ground behind trees, logs, rocks, or any shelter that was nearest.

Extra #5

33.9747, -84.7607
Renter's house location at the corner of the Pickett's Mill and Leverett's Mill Roads

Position yourself in front of the small fenced in area along the road. You should be facing north. This small area between here and the crossroads to your right was a small farm rented out by the Picketts to an unknown family. The edge of the large wheat field is just a short distance away in front. The Confederate trenches of Govan's Brigade would have been in that area. The modern park often builds up a log barricade in that location to mark the spot, and it may be visible as well. Standing here in 1864, you would have been just behind the main Confederate line.

The fenced area in front of you could have been a small cellar for the farm, or another well. A short distance to your right is another boarded up platform. This is the well for the farm, and is similar to the well found at station Blue #4 (page 23). To the right of the well can be found a mound of stones, the remains of the chimney.

When the Confederate army arrived, the family that lived here fled. However, they made an attempt to hide their belongings. Lieutenant R.M. Collins of the 6th & 15th Texas in Granbury's Brigade was stationed just behind you in a supporting line. He later recalled, "our line was on a ridge; in our front was quite a farm, the farmhouse was empty, and the family before leaving seemed to have made some effort to store away in safe places their household goods. We found a feather bed and several other articles in an old well. All this time way to our left the booming of cannon and the roar of small arms could be heard."

Turn right and walk back to White #1. Then turn left or north to continue along the White Loop.

White #2
33.9772, -84.7594
Looking south toward Govan's Brigade.

From the White #2 station marker, walk off the Leverett's Mill Road to the edge of the field and face to the west. Ignore the station marker and its arrow indicator in this instance. It's acceptable to leave the trail here to walk to the field. In 1864, this field was larger than its modern appearance. Lengthwise, to your left and right, it is about the correct distance. However, looking straight ahead it as twice as wide as it is now.

If you look to your left, you will see the southern end of the field. Govan's Brigade held the line there, and the Georgia red clay earthworks would have been visible. Look to your right, or south. General Nathaniel C. McLean's Union brigade was supposed to position itself at the southern edge of the field where you are looking. They were to engage Govan and generally make a lot of noise and make their presence known to discourage any Confederates from moving out and striking Wood's division in the flank. McLean did not move forward and failed in his mission.

This is also the approximate location where the 15th Ohio entered the field during Gibson's advance. After taking fire from in front and their right, they sent Company A forward as skirmishers and bent half the regiment back to refuse their flank. If you have an ancestor in the 15th, they would have witnessed quite the drill gymnastics as they bent too far back, and then were ordered to resume the advance. In their haste to move out, the right wing ended up on the left of the regiment, and the left wing became the new right wing! Lieutenant Alexis Cope, the regiment's adjutant wrote they advanced with, "the left wing of our regiment on the right of our colors, and the right wing on their left. The writer, who was then adjutant of the regiment, confesses to a momentary fit of complete demoralization over its disorganized condition when it went into action. But there was no diminution in the courage of the men in the ranks…"

Extra #6
33.9778, -84.7591
Leverett's Mill Road

You are now at the southern end of the large wheat field where the Leverett's Mill Road entered the woods in 1864. If you are not using GPS, try to orient on the edge of the field through the woods to your left. These woods immediately to your left would have been open field. General Howard moved along this road from the north near this spot. From here he could see Govan's Confederate earthworks at the far end. It was here that he concluded that he had reached the end of the enemy line. He decided to attack their open flank which he thought he could reach by moving through the woods to your right. Unknown to him, there is a large ravine between this location and the enemy flank, and Granbury's Brigade would extend the Confederate line at the last minute.

Near here occurred an incident that illustrates some of the challenges faced by historians when they try to piece together or corroborate a story. Captain Harry M. Stinson on General Howard's staff was wounded while observing the Confederate line across an open field. Generals Howard, Wood, and Johnson remember the incident with slightly different variations. Howard remembers Stinson, "stepped boldly into the opening. He had a new field glass, and here was an excellent opportunity to try it… Stinson had hardly raised his glass to his forehead when a bullet struck him. The missile had penetrated his lungs and made its way entirely through his body." Johnson wrote he, "stepped in between us [Howard and Johnson] and took the glass, and was sweeping the woods beyond the field, when suddenly I heard two distinct reports… Young Stinson reeled and fell. The ball passed through him and buried itself in an oak-tree in his rear. It was the striking of the tree which made the second report." Yet Wood remembered they were actually hiding in the brush and Stinson, "seated himself immediately to my left. In doing so he carelessly rustled the foliage. Instantly there was a sharp crack of a musket; I heard the dead thud of the ball, looked to my left, and saw the young man prone on his back." Even more curiously, neither Howard nor Wood mention Johnson being present!

Extra #7

33.9787, -84.7584
Unknown house along the Leverett's Mill Road.
The mound in the foreground is a pile of stone. Likely a chimney.
The wire fence surrounds a well.

Physical evidence and eyewitness accounts point to the existence of a small house at this location in 1864 and during the battle. Nothing is known about its occupants or owners, although this land was owned by the Pickett family at the time. There are mounds of cut stone, which indicate foundations or a chimney, and there is a well on the site that has been capped for safety.

The regimental history of the 15th Ohio mentions a house at this spot. The 15th marched through here on the way to the large wheat field farther down the Leverett's Mill Road.

> We finally came to an open timbered space, near a road which wound up a hill toward the enemy's supposed position, and came to a halt on the right of the road. There was a house to the left of the road where it began to climb the hill… [after the repulse] It was then growing dark. Failing to find the Fifteenth Ohio, the adjutant went to the rear and found it gathering together its scattered remnants, near the house we noticed when we were resting just before the attack.

White #3
33.9796, -84.7586
Earthworks at the salient.

King's brigade of Regular Army soldiers occupied the area from around station White #4 (pg. 43) to Pickett's Mill Creek. They provided a covering force for the retreating assault units and began constructing earthworks to fortify their position. Their division commander, Brigadier General Richard Johnson, did not like his line and though it was in a bad location, but thought it couldn't be helped as it was dictated by circumstance. The end of his line was below this hill to your left, roughly at a 90 degree angle from the Leverett's Mill Road at White #4. Unfortunately, Confederate skirmishers soon occupied the high ground on the hill you are on now, leaving the Union soldiers in the works on the slope below in a precarious situation.

Plans were made to take the hill and fortify it. On the night of May 29th, those plans were carried out. Companies A and C of the 16th United States Infantry charged uphill into the darkness from your left and drove away the Confederate pickets. Immediately the 2nd Battalion of the 18th United States Infantry moved forward and began digging in, with the two companies of the 16th moving farther forward to cover them. As Captain William J. Fetterman of the 18th United States described it,

> On the night of the 29th the battalion was ordered to advance to a commanding position, then occupied by the enemy's pickets, in front of the right of the brigade, and to throw up a work in the form of a crescent, refusing both its flanks, so as to be as near the main line as possible. The enemy's skirmishers having first been pushed back by the skirmishers of the Sixteenth Infantry, the battalion advanced and carried out the order; working all night under an artillery fire, and by morning had completed the work sufficiently to render it tenable; the next day the work was thoroughly finished. On the 31st the enemy made a determined attack in force on the work, but was repulsed with heavy loss, the battalion sustained a loss of Lieutenant Adair, wounded, and 33 enlisted men.

White #4

33.9801, -84.7576

Wood's division formed here for the May 27th attack, facing to the right.

To your left and right are earthworks built after the battle. This is roughly the right of the line held by King's large Regular Army brigade. From here and to your left, Companies A and C of the 16th United States Infantry launched their night assault to capture the knoll behind you at station White #3 (page 42).

After retiring from the battle, Wood's division took a position farther back, about 300-1,000 yards to your left front in an area not accessible to the public. Life here during static warfare was anything but safe. Artillery fire and shells exploding overhead were common. When the two main lines could not see each other directly skirmishers were sent into the space in between. They often engaged in their own private wars, and casualties mounted daily. Add to that the merciless sun, and sometimes Georgia summer thunderstorms, and life in the trenches was miserable. It was a never-ending, confusing nightmare.

Even commanding officers were not immune. The story below, found in the history of the 15th Ohio and unfolding somewhere along Wood's line deeper in the forest, shows how even the night was no reprieve from the stress and confusion of battle.

> Quite an alarm occurred during the night [the night of May 28/29], the whole brigade being called to arms by the stentorian voice of Colonel Gibson, who had heard (or imagined) some unusual noise, and there was a general uproar all through the camp. There was very little firing, but men were rushing here and there, some yelling at the tops of their voices, evidently just roused from sleep and imagining the whole rebel army right upon us. It was soon known that it was only an unreasonable panic and was caused by a disordered dream of Colonel Gibson.... It was a long time before the buzz of the men's voices and the firing which broke out to our left subsided sufficiently to permit one to sleep.

Extra #8
33.9810, -84.7573
Old Leverett's Mill Road

The Leverett's Mill Road continues ahead of you, but then angles to the left and has since been largely overgrown. A post-war trail continues along this path to the right down to the creek. It was once part of the park's trail system, but is now closed to the public. Along the mill road and about 150 yards ahead over the hill was a field hospital built behind the lines to care for the wounded. Here the injured would be stabilized and prepared for the trip to larger facilities farther back. Those unlucky few who perished from their wounds at the hospital were buried nearby, some of their grave sites discovered during archeological excavations in the 1970s.

Francis A. Keine's experience was typical. Wounded in front of Granbury's Texans in the ravine fighting with the 89th Illinois, he describes his journey to the hospital behind the lines.

> After gitting a little further back I came to where our men were establishing a new line… and started for the rear in search of a hospital where I could git my arm dressed. Troops were fast coming… all in the best of spirits… after walking some distance I got to the Division field hospital, here after waiting some time I got my arm bound up… A few rebel shells past over us as we were waiting for our turn at the doctors creating a greateal of bustle and confusion although we were generally safe being in a deep gully. After I succeeded in gitting some warm coffee I started for the General Hospital wich was said to be half a mile off… I found it rather a long walk being fatigued and bleeding very freely all the time and the distance being instid of half a mile not less than 5 miles… About one oclock I got to the hospital so weak that I could hardly lift one foot before the other.

White #5
33.9803, -84.7572
Union battery position built after the May 27th battle.

    Howard's flank march was made without any artillery. There were no roads on which wheeled vehicles could travel, and artillery would have simply slowed them down. However, once the battle on the 27th was over and the men had to dig in, artillery support was desperately needed General Howard that night ordered the engineers and pioneers to begin cutting down trees and building a road to his new position. This opened up access to wheeled vehicles including artillery, commissary wagons, and ambulances to carry the wounded farther to the rear.

    The four horseshoe shaped earthworks to your right were built the night of the 27th and protected a four gun battery. The next day they began firing at the Confederate artillery across the way. When you continue along the trail, notice the infantry earthworks as you cross the footbridge over them.

Continue to Station Blue #9 (page 28) where the Blue, White, and Red Loops merge and continue the tour from there.

The Red Loop

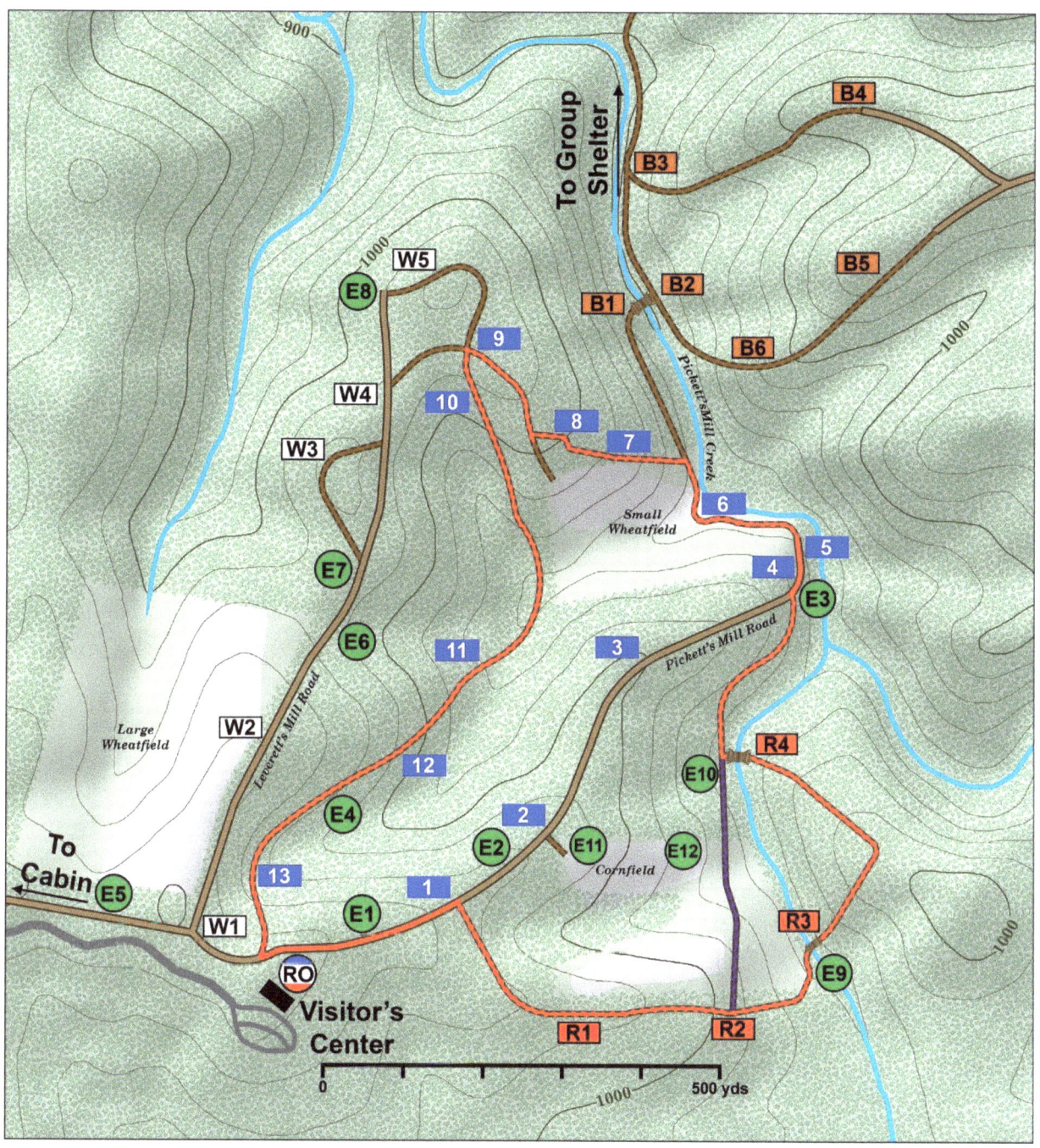

Ravine Overlook
33.9742, -847590

Stand on the elevated observation platform and look north. The wartime Pickett's Mill Road will be in front of you going left to right. You are standing at the left end of Granbury's Brigade. We don't know the exact order of each regiment in the brigade line, but this section was likely held by the 7th and 10th Texas regiments. Govan's Brigade would be to your left. Key's section of two 12 lb. howitzers would have been at the top of the hill to your left at the intersection of the Pickett's Mill and Leverett's Mill Roads.

Along this section and in this area, Major John R. Kennard of the 10th Texas walked along the line encouraging his men. "Put your trust in God, men. For He is with us." However, he couldn't resist taunting the enemy, and took up the cry "Come on—we are demoralized!" Almost immediately, a Union ball struck him in the head, and he fell. It was a serious but not life threatening wound. Raising himself up, Kennard exclaimed, "Boys, I told them a lie—and I believe that is the reason I got shot."

The Union approached this position from the opposite slope straight ahead. Colonel Gibson's brigade was heavily engaged with Granbury, Govan, and Key at this section of the line.

To walk the Blue or Red Loops, turn right and follow the road to the next stations. To hike the White Loop, turn left. Even if you do not plan on hiking the White Loop, you might benefit from walking the short distance to the station White #1 (page 37) just a short distance away and reading about Key's howitzers. Then return here to the Overlook and continue on another loop.

Extra #1
33.9746, -84.7585
Looking up toward the Confederate line from the Union perspective.
Taken off trail with park permission.

If you stop at some point in-between the Ravine Overlook and the Blue #1 station, you will find yourself in the middle of Granbury's brigade line. Turn to the left and face north, then walk to the edge of the trail so that you can look into the woods. Granbury's line was only a few yards into the trees. You can make out only 20 or 30 yards away where the slope drops off sharply into the ravine. When the Hazen's Union line fully crested this precipice, the Texans opened fire at point blank range. Hundreds of men fell in the initial volley, then both sides took cover. This repeated when Gibson's brigade charged through Hazen's men during their attempt to dislodge the Confederates.

William Oliphant of the 6th & 15th Texas Cavalry (dismounted) remembered a scene years later. During Gibson's attack, the 32nd Indiana charged this portion of the line, or perhaps a little to the right. The 32nd was largely recruited from Leavensburg, and Oliphant lived there as a young boy until his family moved to Texas. According to Oliphant,

> The color-bearer of the regiment fell with his colors, instantly another seized the flag and held it aloft only to fall dead. Again and again it was raised until six brave men yielded their lives in trying to keep it flying. The sixth man fell with the flag in front of our company only about ten or twelve feet from us… When the Indiana regiment broke and fell back leaving the flag on the ground at our feet one of the federals turned and seeing it was being left behind threw down his gun, came back and picked it up. He straightened himself to his full height, gritted his teeth and flapped his flag in our faces. Instantly a half dozen rifles were leveled on him…but just then one of our boys cried out, "don't shoot him, he's too brave." We lowered our rifles and gave him a cheer as he carried his flag safely away.

Oliphant would later learn that the flag was made by his aunt, who remained in Lawrenceburg.

Blue #1
33.9747, -84.7577
Granbury's line from the Confederate perspective.

You are near the right end of Granbury's brigade. The Pickett's Mill Road continues ahead. The Red Loop trail to your right was not present during the battle. Here the 6th & 15th Texas Cavalry (dismounted) anchored the end of the line. It stretched along the slope in to your left, and curved around in front of you across the road. It likely bent back and touched or crossed the road facing east. It primarily fought the 124th Ohio a short distance away.

From here, the Confederates could see Hazen's second line crossing the road farther downhill and getting into a position to flank them, or get behind the army. General Granbury sent messengers for help, and Govan sent the 8th & 19th Arkansas regiment. They arrived, formed to the right of the Texans (to your right and behind you), and led by their previous commander Brigadier John H. Kelly, charged into the 5th Kentucky at the cornfield. Several of the right companies of the 6th & 15th charged with them. Their efforts, along with the arrival of Lowrey's Brigade, saved the Confederate right.

Captain Sebron Sneed of the 6th & 15th later relayed an amusing anecdote to his wife in a letter,
> The right of our regiment also charged the flankers and they retreated. Our boys took a few prisoners in the charge. We were getting nearly out of ammunition, the men having fired 50 rounds each. I scared one Yankee awfully. I had a large butcher knife in my hand that I had been using to cut a cartridge Box from one of the wounded men in order to give his ammunition to the others. I had just finished when Sam Piper came to me with a prisoner he had captured. I ran to him with the knife reased to cut his cartridge box off. The poor devil thought I intended to kill him and threw up his hands with the most pitiful face. I could not restrain a laugh at his despairing countenance.

Red #1
33.9739, -84.7554
The southern edge of the cornfield.

You are looking down the fence line held by Confederate cavalry on this side of the cornfield. It was described by at least one participant as an "old cornfield" so was probably not planted at the time of the battle, yet recognizable as a cornfield by the mound patterns used in 19th Century farming. The field was about the same size to your left. In winter you can see across the field to the other side. However, in 1864 the cornfield extended all the way to the small stream in front of you, today called Wildcat Branch. Of course, it's not visible from here, but the wood line ahead was farther away.

As Hazen's second line advanced to this fence, moving from your left to right, the Confederate cavalry fought to buy time for reinforcements to arrive. The Federals gained much of the fence in front of you, but the rebels held this corner. The 8th & 19th Arkansas charged into the flank of the 5th Kentucky down in the ravine to your left. Lowrey's Brigade ran past your right, stretching around the cornfield, surrounding it on three sides.

Captain Charles C. Briant of the 6th Indiana wrote,

> Captain Samuel McKeehan, who was our acting Major… told the writer to go down where Colonel Berry [commander of the 5th Kentucky] was, in the woods, and tell him to charge up and take the rebel line on his front, or we would be compelled to fall back. I instant turned to the right and started in a quick run, quartering to the rear, thinking Colonel Berry was about in that direction. I had gone about one hundred feet, which brought me directly in front of the rebels, who still held their line on our right, when one of them fired at me as I ran, but I was going a little too fast. The ball plowed across the small of the back, but not deep enough to cripple; so after turning a somersault, and going through some other gymnastic performances, I bounded off down the hill, found the Colonel and delivered my message, and, with all possible speed, made my way back to my post in the regiment…

Red #2

33.9741, -84.7537

Looking along Confederate trenches build after the May 27th battle.

If you are facing along the arrow on the Red #2 station marker, you will see woods ahead and the cornfield is behind you. Confederate cavalry was fighting along the southern fence line to your left and right. The 6th Indiana captured the fence to your right, and the 23rd Kentucky the fence to your left. Lowrey's Brigade, rushed here by General Cleburne as reinforcements, circled around the field in the woods in front of you. William. E. Sloane of the 5th Tennessee Cavalry describes being pushed back and then counterattacking along with Lowrey's men.

> The enemy never attempted a charge, but moved forward very slowly until we checked him up, and then he stood still, all the time pouring forth a volcano of fire as I never saw before. They must have mistaken our numbers, or else they would have made a charge and run right over us. They outnumbered us at least twelve to one, for they had six lines of two ranks each, while we had only one single rank line, and in some places it was stretched out into a mere skirmish line. We were told to hold our position until reinforcements arrived, and we did it, though they were a long time coming. At last a part of Cleburne's division of infantry moved up in our rear in line of battle, and infantry and cavalry mixed together in one line. Then a roar went up which those Yankees could probably hear despite the noise of their own guns, at least if they could not hear it they could see it and feel it too. After that the battle was short, the enemy soon retreated and the field was ours.

After the fighting on the 27th Lowrey's men began to build earthworks. Cleburne's Division was ordered away to rejoin their corps closer to Dallas, and the position was occupied by Hindman's Division of Hood's Corps. While their main line and earthworks were located here, generally following the Red Loop back to station Blue #2, their skirmish line was on the ridge behind you along the Pickett's Mill Road. This location is discussed at station Blue #3 (page 59).

The short Purple Trail is behind you. It travels through what was then the open cornfield and is a shortcut to station Red #4 (page 55). To follow the Red Loop, turn left and continue downhill.

Extra #9

33.9747, -84.7529
The cornfield's southeast fence corner.

Face west looking uphill. You are near the approximate location of the southeast fence corner. The 23rd Kentucky reached this part of the fence, and the two sides fought each other at point blank range, even through the same fence! Sergeant Arnold Brandley of the 23rd later wrote this detailed recollection of the close range fighting along this fence and the corner here.

> What a shower of bullets met us! We fought each other through that fence… I loaded and fired so fast my gun-barrel grew dangerously hot. A ball struck a rock, glanced, then hit me on the foot near the instep. It made me dance; then maddened me. I forgot the heated gun-barrel. I fired away, not more than 100 from the Johnnies. While loading, a ball hit my gun just above the lower band, smashing it flat. It saved my life. I picked up a dead comrade's gun.
>
> The rebels we had been firing at were located behind a pair of bars [fence rails] a few yards to our left; they had stuck rocks and chunks between the bars as a protection to themselves. From some cause they failed to notice us on their flank, as they always looked across the field to where, I am informed, the 57th Ind. [6th Kentucky] held a position.
>
> We finally crowded our enemy behind the bars; none showed their heads any longer, we made up a squad and charged the bars. I saw enough to make my blood run cold; plenty of dead men, with a very lively line behind them [Lowrey's men moving into position]. We hastily fired into them and hastily retreated; not before they shot most of the squad. They now located us. Some of them go over the fence and were making their way under the brow of the hill we occupied, so as to gain our rear…

Lowrey's Brigade ran to the hill behind you and encircled the cornfield, trapping the Union regiments there on three sides.

Red #3
33.9751, -84.7530
Looking along Wildcat Branch toward the cornfield.

Face toward the arrow looking uphill. Two regiments of Lowrey's Brigade, the 32nd and 45th Mississippi, climbed the hill in front of you and turned to your left. From that position, they fronted the eastern edge of the cornfield. From there, they were on the flank of Hazen's second line in the field. The Federal 23rd Kentucky was at the fence on the southern edge, and the 6th Kentucky was behind them, protecting their flank. Captain Isaac N. Johnston, commanding the 6th wrote,

> …while part of the Twenty-Third Kentucky, and the right wing of the Sixth Kentucky was formed diagonally across it, and the left wing of the Sixth was formed front to rear to meet a flanking column of the enemy that was moving to our rear. This movement on the part of the enemy would have been successful had I not at that moment formed my left wing so as to return the flanking fire he was already pouring into us.

The Confederates charged the cornfield from three sides. Charles C. Briant of the 6th Indiana, after his run described at station Red #1 (page 51) saw the Confederates massing on the flanks and saw that the rebel column had,

> … passed by our own left, down the creek, and were just coming into he field at the mouth of the ravine, and in five minutes more time would have been completely in our rear. I instantly gave the command to retreat, and at eth same time, with all possible speed, went back up to my own regiment, yelling at the top of my voice all the way up, "Retreat! Retreat!" and as soon as I arrive at my own regiment and company gave the order, "Retreat square to the rear or we will be captured." It is needless to say that both regiments broke in wild disorder for a place of safety.

Red #4
33.9765, -84.7536
Scribner's position from the Confederate cavalry's viewpoint.

You are looking from the vantage point of the Confederate cavalry toward Colonel Scribner's position. The Confederates were forced to fall back from the ridge above you, and Scribner's men took up a defensive position at the top. To your left, and behind you, Hazen's second line was fighting in the cornfield. The cavalry on the hill you just walked down could fire into the flank of Hazen's men, and together with Lowrey's infantry brigade, pushed them back. Scribner, however, would not be moved. However, they would also not advance.

Andrew Jackson Williams of the 2nd Tennessee Cavalry described some of the fighting in this area,

> General Wheeler and his staff was near our part of the line and he commenced sending staff officers and couriers in both directions… our line in our field had hard fighting to reestablish on our left [the cornfield].
>
> Captain Turner and a few others crossed our breastworks and went down on the side of the ridge where we could see the fighting and our men driving the Yankees. Captain order(ed) our line to advance and the men crossed the breastworks, charged the Yankees down the ridge. In our front was timber and we could not see the enemy in our front until we had some distance down the ridge. When we was some 75 or 100 yards from the breastworks, they fired a volley into us that killed and wounded quite a number of our men.
>
> Captain Turner was slightly wounded in the hip and was standing near me. He started over toward me and I thought he was going to fall. I put my hand and caught him but he soon said he was not bad hurt and I turned him loose. At about that time Lieutenant Tate Shull was shot down, and one of his thighs broke. Dock Webb and Ike Barnett had started to take him off the field when Captain Turner saw them and ordered me to help them carry him off. They each one had him by the shoulder and I took him by the pant leg and we carried him back up the ridge.

Extra #10

33.9762, -84.7536
Looking south toward cornfield.
Purple Trail to Red #2 is to the left.

After crossing the bridge walking from station Red #4, turn left and face south.

You are standing in between Scribner's brigade, behind you at the top of the hill, and Knefler's brigade, in front of you about 50 to 75 yards ahead. You should be able to see the open cornfield to your right front. During the war, the cornfield in front extended all the way to the creek. Look to your left front, where you just left Station Red #4 (page 55). Confederate fire from the cavalry on the hill could fire straight down into the flank of the Union soldiers stationed along the cornfield to your front. This caused quite a few casualties among the Union soldiers there, mostly from the 9th and 17th Kentucky regiments.

Colonel Alexander M. Stout of the 17th wrote in his report after the battle,

> The enemy were in their front across a small field with rail barricades, and also upon a considerable ridge on the left of the ravine before mentioned, which commanded pretty much the position of the whole brigade… The fire from that ridge was incessant and very destructive. A brigade of the First Division, Fourteenth Army Corps, commanded by Colonel Scribner, was on my left and part of it on the left of the ravine, but as their skirmish line was not advanced as far to the front as my line of battle, it therefore could not or did not drive the enemy from that ridge or protect us from cross-fires. I tried to induce the officer commanding the regiment in the first line on the left of the ravine of that brigade to advance as far to the front as our line, but could not move him. I then tried Colonel Scribner, but failed. In obedience to orders from the colonel commanding the brigade, I moved my regiment to the left and to the ravine; and the Ninth Regiment Kentucky Volunteers, which was in the second line, came to my assistance. Darkness came, and the men of the two regiments became thoroughly intermingled. Our own firing was rapid; that of the enemy destructive.

Extra #3
33.9777, -84.7530
Looking north from Scribner's position toward the attacking Confederate cavalry.
Taken off the trail with park permission.

Position yourself at the intersection of the Blue and Red Loops. Look south with the Red Loop in front of you.

When Scribner's brigade advanced it passed the Pickett farm and field behind you, ascended the ridge, and took position here. You are at the left flank of the 37th Indiana. The 78th Pennsylvania was farther down the ridge to your right. Both regiments were south of the road in the woods along the crest. Many of the soldiers in these two regiments picked up and carried logs and fence rails as they advanced. This was not the mindset of an aggressive force bent on charging the enemy. When the two regiments reached this location they dropped their cargo and used it for cover. In this position the two regiments fought for several hours against repeated attacks to your front by Confederate cavalry and infantry.

Look to your left. When Scribner first arrived Confederate cavalry along the heights across the creek put a heavy fire into the left flank of the 37th Indiana. Because of this, Colonel Scribner decided to send half of his brigade across the creek to push the cavalrymen back and secure his position. This decision, coupled with the Confederate attacks up the slope in front of you, delayed any attempt to advance and help Hazen's men in the cornfield about 150 yards to your right front.

John J. Kirk of the 37th picked up a rotten log during the advance. His friend John Withrow mocked him, but Kirk predicted, "You will be glad to get your head behind this log before long." Sure enough, as soon as the firing started Withrow was beside him. "You made fun of me for carrying this chunk, and just as I said, you were the first man to get behind it." Suddenly a ball came through the log, striking Kirk in the face. Wounded, but not fatally, Kirk made is way to the rear. When Withrow's gun malfunctioned, he took Kirk's abandoned rifle and continued the fight.

You now have a choice. If you wish to continue along the Red Loop, turn around, face north, and continue along the Pickett's Mill Road toward station Blue #4 (page 23). From there, follow the Blue Loop and stations from that page.

If you wish for more information about the fight at the cornfield, and a shorter hike back to the Visitor's Center, turn to your right and continue down the Pickett's Mill Road to station Blue #3 at the next page.

Blue #3
33.9773, -84.7542
Confederate rifle pit.

    This section of the ridge was held by the Confederate cavalry as they attempted to slow down the Union advance. The cavalrymen were posted in a skirmish line. This was a loose formation with the men spaced several yards apart. On the offensive, a skirmish line was used to gain information on the enemy and report it back up the chain of command, giving the generals a better idea of what was going on. On the defensive they kept the enemy away from the main line and prevented enemy skirmishers from gaining any information. During an attack, they served as an early warning system for those behind them so they weren't taken by surprise, and did their best to slow down the enemy advance.

    This last role is what the Confederate cavalry attempted to do against the oncoming Union infantry during the battle on May 27th. They were stationed along the ridge to your left, stretching in front of and behind you as far as you can see. Scribner's brigade pushed them back in this area, and Hazen's men forced them to retreat behind you.

    The shallow depression to your immediate left is a rifle pit, used for protection against enemy fire. There is a line of them along the north side of the road. Today it would be called a foxhole. There is a strong likelihood this rifle pit and others along the ridge were built and manned by Confederate infantry the week after the battle. The Confederate cavalry did not have time to dig them on May 27th. The infantry skirmishers here kept watch on King's brigade to the north. You can see the opposite end of the small wheat field during the winter. Confederate rifle fire from these skirmishers caused many casualties in the Union ranks across the ravine.

    In front of you to your right was the approximate location of the right flank of the 78th Pennsylvania as they fought on this ridge during the May 27th battle.

Blue #2
33.9753, -84.7561
Union approach toward the Cornfield along the Pickett's Mill Road.

As you walked along Pickett's Mill Road from Station Blue #3 you passed through the area held by Company A of the 74th Ohio as they protected the right flank of Scribner's brigade during the night.

From this station, Hazen's second line surged out of the woods to your left after pushing back the cavalry skirmishers trying to slow them down. Crossing the road you are standing in, the Federals reached the northern edge of the cornfield to your right and continued beyond. The attack at the cornfield offered the best chance of success during the battle. General Hazen established his headquarters near a tree across the road to your right. From there, he commanded his brigade and tried to coordinate the two wings.

Colonel Knefler's second line also exited the ravine here and crossed the road on the way to the cornfield. Here Lieutenant Marcus Woodcock of the 9th Kentucky remarked how many of Hazen's retiring soldiers turned around and joined them in the attack,

> We met the gallant but defeated heroes of the front lines just as we commenced ascending the hill. They presented all marks of a defeated, badly cut up, but unwhipped force; and they met us with cheers and exhortations and invectives on the rebels that would have reassure the minds of any but the most timid, and hundreds of them joined our ranks and returned to the contest.

From there, they advanced and drove the 4th Louisiana from its advanced position at the northern edge of the cornfield.

Extra #11

33.9751, -84.7555
Looking east along the northern edge of the cornfield.

Orient yourself east by facing to the left once you enter the cornfield from the trail. This cornfield was an important location during the battle, and the fighting here could have turned the tide in the Union's favor. What information is available from contemporary sources describes it as an "old cornfield," so it's possible, if not likely, that there was no corn planted during the battle.

From the fence line on the northern edge of the field, often reconstructed by the park but sometimes absent, the second line of Hazen's brigade launched its attack with the regiments moving from left to right. They also rallied at this fence after they were repulsed and halted their counter-attackers. It was also at this corner of the field where you are standing that the 4th Louisiana, charging uphill from your right, reached the fence and engaged in hand-to-hand combat with the defenders. If you walk into the field to the military crest you will then be standing in the approximate location where the 19th Ohio and 79th Indiana set up a temporary rail barricade and fought until nightfall.

After the battle, near this location, a member in the 4th Louisiana found a letter in the personal effects of a fallen Union soldier. We'll never know if, after the battle, he was returned home as he wished, or if he is one of the more than 10,000 known or unknown buried in the nearby Marietta National Cemetery.

> "Dearest Darling, Alice, 27th May, 1864: I take this time to write on a rest. We are marching hard to flank the rebels from Atlanta. I know not where we are in this harsh country. The inhabitants are very poor and ignorant creatures. We expect a fight soon. I suspect we will teach the secesh a lesson. If my life should end, my only wish is that I not be buried in this traitorous land…"

Extra #12
33.9752 -84.7541
Looking west along the northern edge of the cornfield.

    Walk along the northern edge of the cornfield until you reach the opposite corner. Be aware of tall grass and ticks, and stick close to the tree line. Turn to the right and face south. You will be looking across the field, not back the way you came like the image above.

    From here, Hazen launched his attack across the cornfield with his second line. In 1864 the open cornfield extended to your left all the way down to the creek. So during the battle, you would actually have been standing along the fence near the middle of the field.

    The 5th Kentucky was stalled to your far right at the bottom of the swale in front. It was being attacked by the 8th & 19th Arkansas and 33rd Alabama. The 6th Indiana advanced to your front, the 23rd Kentucky to its left, and the 6th Kentucky behind the 23rd. While the gained the opposite fence (much more visible in the winter), they were soon counterattacked by cavalry and Lowrey's Brigade of infantry from the front and the high ground to your left. The Federals fell back here, rallied at the fence, and forced the pursuing Confederates back to the southern fence. The fighting then settled into a long range shooting match until the 4th Louisiana charged the fence line to your right. They were initially successful after a hand-to-hand fight, but Knefler's brigade soon arrived and drove them back across the field.

    At your current location, the 9th and 17th Kentucky intermingled and fought from this fence. They fought the Confederates on the other side of the field, but also received enemy fire from the hill across the creek to your left. This flanking fire caused the Union so much trouble that the 17th's commander went back to Scribner's brigade to your left rear and asked them to move their skirmishers forward to drive them away. Scribner refused as described at station Extra #10 (page 29).

The Orange (Brand House) Loop

Access to the Orange Loop is through the Blue Loop. Beginning at the Ravine Overlook, follow the Blue Loop to station Blue #6. Continue along the loop until the next crossroads. Continue straight. When you return from the Orange Loop, turn right and continue along the Blue Loop.

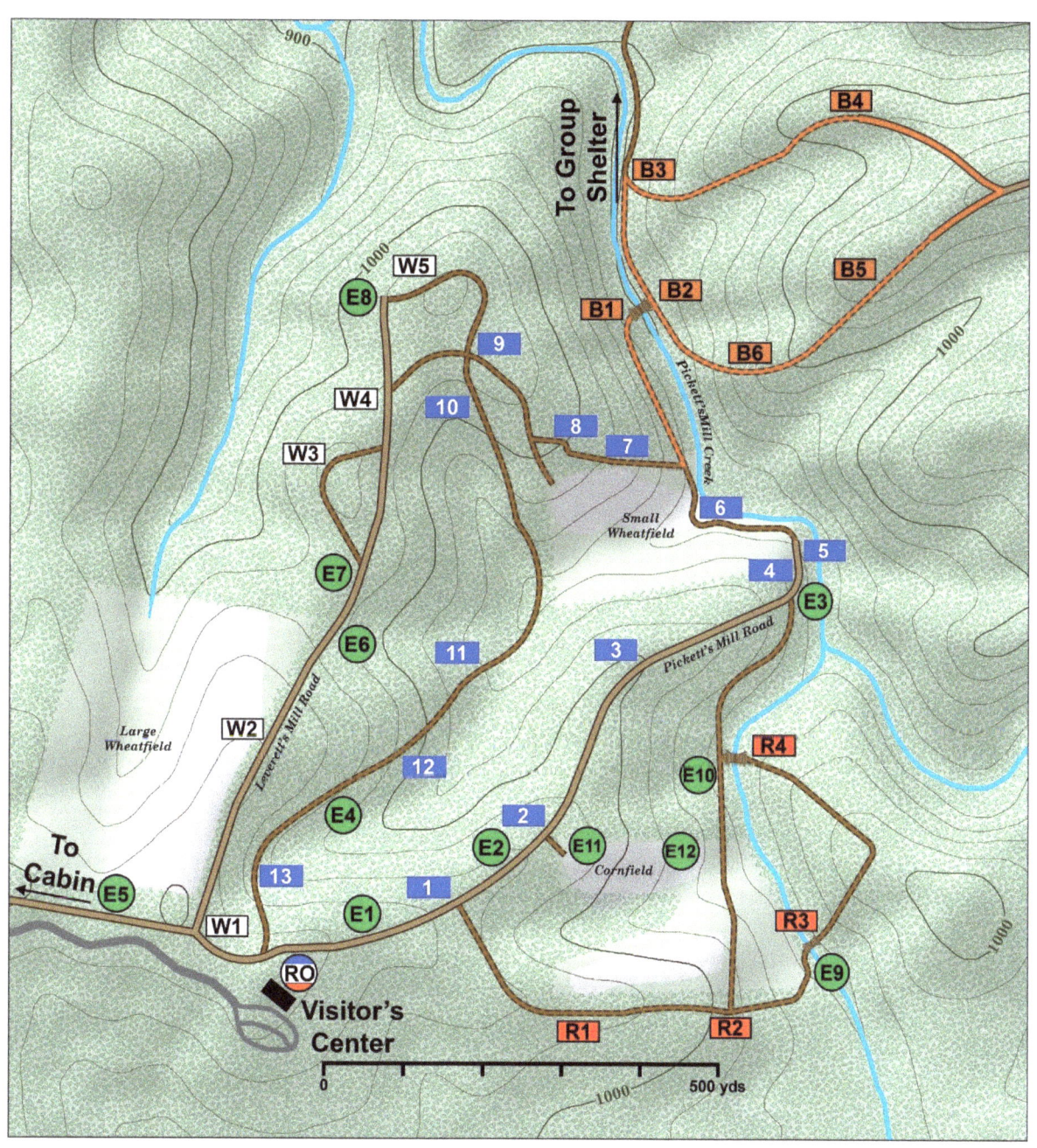

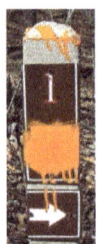

Brand #1
33.9810, -84.7552
The area just behind the Union lines.

This was an area of considerable activity on and during the week following May 27th. During the battle on May 27th, the hill behind you was crowded with men from King's and Carlin's brigades held in reserve. When King moved to the front, Carlin's men remained. At about 11 pm Carlin was ordered to cross Pickett's Mill Creek in front of you and extend the line to protect against an enemy attack in that area. Later in the night Scribner's brigade fell back to this area to regroup. They would help reinforce both King and Carlin during the next week.

This area was safer than the trenches at the front line, but not necessarily "safe." During the morning of May 28th, Union soldiers decide it was a good time to make the fuel on which the army ran; coffee. Soon numerous small fires sprang up in the ravine to your left and rear. Unfortunately, the smoke rising from this area soon drew the attention of Confederate artillery. Division commander Richard Johnson recalled,

> At this time King and myself were sitting on the stone which we had used for a pillow, with our faces buried in our hands and our hands on our knees. Suddenly the enemy opened with one or more batteries upon our position. I straightened myself up in time to see the effect of the first shot, which was to cut a soldier into two pieces; the second shot carried away the arm of Colonel Niebling, of Ohio [21st Ohio]; the third shot grazed the talma of King and struck me just over the liver and disabled me. I was taken back to a safe place and King assumed command of the division. If he had had the same amount of curiosity that I exhibited he would have received the twelve pound shell instead of myself.

Brand #2

33.9811, -84.7546
Looking up the slope where the left of Carlin's brigade was stationed.

Just before midnight on May 27th Carlin's brigade moved across the creek near station Brand #3 (page 66). The next day, the left of the brigade advanced to this ridge and dug in. On subsequent days the brigade advanced to the next ridge south at stations Brand # 5 (page 68) and #6 (page 69). Unfortunately, there is not a lot of primary material available for the actions on this sector of the line, so exact troop movements are difficult to interpret.

Brand #3
33.9823, -84.7548
The area behind the Union lines.

    If you look to your right, you will be looking across Pickett's Mill Creek toward the rear of the Union lines. This area would be bustling with a myriad of behind-the-lines activities in the week following the battle; aid stations, commissary and food preparation, as well as ammunition distribution. Regiments not on the front lines and held in reserve would also have been stationed in this area, likely with tents. A luxury they didn't get on the front lines.

    About 250 yards straight northeast of here is the site of the J. C. Leverett house and mill. Leverett purchased the property from Ben Pickett in 1862. Unlike the food-based grist mill operated by Benjamin and Martha Pickett, Leverett's mill was described as a "woolen mill or factory." Leverett sold the property in 1867. The remains of the house and mill dam still exist, but are currently off limits.

    When Carlin's brigade first crossed the creek near this location before midnight on the 27th, they took up a position on the ridge to your left. The next day, the left of the brigade advanced to the next ridge south.

Brand #4
33.9828, -84.7517
The Brand House

    This is the location of the Brand house. The mound in front of you is the remains of the main hearth, or chimney. Zachariah Brand purchased 120 acres on this ridge between 1850 and 1860. The Brand and Pickett families reportedly had a long history together, having known each other from Fairfield County, South Carolina. At the time of the battle, Zach Brand was living here with his wife Ann, their unmarried daughters Martha, Celia, Elenor, Nancy, Charity, and Sarah, teenage sons William and John, and the 70-71 year old family patriarch Malachi Brand.

    While not as prosperous as the other farmers and mill owners along Pickett's Mill Creek, Zach was still able to purchase several items from Ben Pickett's estate after his death at the Battle of Chickamauga. This included his horses, male donkey, hogs, shoats, yoke of oxen, wagon, plow, plow stock, beehives, saddles, Colt pistols, and $50 watch.

    Several accounts mention the wide open fields to the east of Carlin's line, which is on the ridge behind you. The area immediately around the farm was almost certainly open and fenced. So in all likelihood, the area to your left was open farmland, possibly all the way to modern GA Hwy 92. Unfortunately, there are no maps of the area from 1864, so its layout is impossible to map. The house itself was almost certainly destroyed during the static operations in the area the week after the battle and never rebuilt.

Brand #5
33.9813, -84.7519
Union rifle pits.

To your right is a Union rifle pit dug to protect the skirmishers from Carlin's brigade. They continue on the right side of the trail as you walk toward station Brand #6. The skirmish lines between the two foes were so close that the Confederate rifle pits are just a few yards to your left down the slope. On the hill across the ravine to your left was the main Confederate infantry line.

One small incident that occurred in this area is mentioned several times across official reports and regimental histories. Captain Robert J. Waggener, brigade assistant adjutant-general (a staff officer/aide position), was establishing and coordinating the position of this skirmish line on the morning of May 28th when he was shot and killed around 10 am. The situation here was very fluid. After all, the battle only ended the previous night, and the units were new to this area and fighting for control of key terrain. Because of this, his body was behind enemy lines for quite some time. A plan was made, and in an 1864 version of leave-no-man-behind the Union soldiers from the 15th Kentucky rushed the enemy and recovered his body.

The 15th's regimental report stated, "At this point Captain Waggener, brigade adjutant-general, was killed early in the day in front of our works. His body was left inside enemy lines until the afternoon, when a detachment from the regiment charged the enemy's line and recovered it."

The regimental history of the 42nd Indiana described the situation here, "The principle lines of the two armies were so close together that when the picket lines were drawn they were not fifty yards apart in the 42d Indiana's immediate front… It was while fixing a picket line to protect the men while at work that the brave Captain Wagner, of General Carlin's staff, was killed, and a fight of half an hour to recover his body followed, and the wounding of several on our side- and we knew not how many of the enemy's."

Brand #6
33.9800, -84.7537
Union earthworks along Carlin's line.

    The earthworks to your right are a continuation of the rifle pits strung out along the ridge east of here toward station Brand #5. They were occupied by soldiers from Carlin's brigade.
    On the evening of May 30th, the Confederates attacked this portion of the line. The attacking unit was Stewart's Division of Hood's Corps. General Carlin described the attack in his report,

> The works along the front of the whole brigade were strengthened this morning. At 6 o'clock this p.m. the right of the brigade, extending from Pumpkin Vine Creek [Pickett's Mill Creek] on the right to Brand's house on the left, was attacked by a part of Hood's corps, which advanced from the rebel works in line of battle. After a brisk engagement of several minutes the enemy fell back with considerable loss, leaving a part of his killed and wounded in our front. The following are the names of the regiments engaged: Tenth Wisconsin, Forty-second Indiana, Twenty-first Wisconsin, and First Wisconsin (Third Brigade).

    Colonel John A. Minter of the 54th Alabama in Brigadier General Alpheus Baker's Brigade, Stewart's Division wrote this in his after battle report describing the action,

> On the evening of the 30th, about 4 o'clock, ordered in front of the works with my regiment to ascertain the position of the enemy if possible. After throwing out skirmishers, advancing about 400 yards in front of the works, encountered the enemy's skirmishers. Drove them from their position about 300 yards, enemy losing 3 killed and, in my opinion, not less than 10 wounded. Finding that we were under an enfilading fire right and left, retired about 100 yards; there remained until sundown, with a loss of 1 killed, 1 missing, 1 wounded and brought in.

The Cabin

33.9748, -84.7642

    The Pickett's Mill Battlefield State Historic Site has a historic log cabin that is open to the public. It was owned by the Prather family and was originally located on Old Stilesboro Road. Built in the 1850s, road expansion threatened it with demolition in the early 21st Century. Instead, it was donated to the state and moved to Pickett's Mill Park in 2002.

    Today the cabin hosts living history events for the park, and is open to the public. You can get a feel for what it was like to live in rural Georgia in the mid-19th Century.

    To get to the cabin, turn left from the Ravine Overlook at the Visitor's Center on the Pickett's Mill Road. Walk past the station White #1 at the intersection with the Leverett's Mill Road and keep going. The cabin is about 400 yards past the crossroads.

Order of Battle

Union

Army of the Cumberland
Fourth Army Corps
Major General Oliver O. Howard

Third Division
Brigadier General Thomas J. Wood

1st Brigade
Colonel William H. Gibson
35th Illinois
89th Illinois
32nd Indiana
15th Ohio
49th Ohio
15th Wisconsin

2nd Brigade
Brigadier General William B. Hazen
6th Indiana
5th Kentucky
6th Kentucky
23rd Kentucky
1st Ohio
41st Ohio
93rd Ohio
124th Ohio

3rd Brigade
Colonel Frederick Knefler
79th Indiana
9th Kentucky
17th Kentucky
13th Ohio
19th Ohio
59th Ohio
86th Indiana

Fourteenth Army Corps
First Division
Brigadier General Richard W. Johnson

1st Brigade
Brigadier General William P. Carlin
104th Illinois
42nd Indiana
88th Indiana
15th Kentucky
2nd Ohio
33rd Ohio
94th Ohio
10th Wisconsin
21st Wisconsin

2nd Brigade
Brigadier General John H. King
11th Michigan
69th Ohio
1st & 3rd Bns 15th U.S.
2nd Bn 15th U.S.
1st Bn. 16th U.S.
2nd Bn. 16th U.S.
1st & 3rd Bns 18th U.S.
2nd Bn. 18th U.S.
1st & 2nd Bns. 19th U.S.

3rd Brigade
Colonel Benjamin F. Scribner
37th Indiana
38th Indiana
21st Ohio
74th Ohio
78th Pennsylvania
1st Wisconsin

Army of the Ohio
Twenty-Third Army Corps
Second Division
<u>1st Brigade</u>
Brigadier General Nathaniel C. McLean
80th Indiana
13th Kentucky
25th Michigan
3rd Tennessee
6th Tennessee

Confederate

Army of Tennessee
Hardee's Corps
Cleburne's Division
Major General Patrick R. Cleburne

<u>Polk's Brigade</u>
Brigadier General Lucius Polk
1st & 15th Arkansas
5th Confederate
2nd Tennessee
48th Tennessee

<u>Govan's Brigade</u>
Brigadier General Daniel C. Govan
2nd & 24th Arkansas
5th & 13th Arkansas
6th & 7th Arkansas
8th & 19th Arkansas
3rd Confederate

<u>Lowrey's Brigade</u>
Brigadier General Mark P. Lowrey
16th Alabama
33rd Alabama
45th Alabama
32nd Mississippi
45th Mississippi

<u>Granbury's Brigade</u>
Brigadier General Hiram B. Granbury
7th Texas
10th Texas
6th Texas & 15th Texas Cavalry (dismounted)
17th & 18th Texas Cavalry (dismounted)
24th & 25th Texas Cavalry (dismounted)

<u>Hotchkiss' Battalion</u>
Key's Arkansas Battery
Semple's Alabama Battery
Warren's Mississippi Battery

Hood's Corps
Hindman's Division
<u>Walthall's Brigade</u>
Brigadier General Edward C. Walthall
24th & 27th Mississippi
29th & 30th Mississippi
34th Mississippi

Army of Mississippi (Polk's Corps)
<u>Quarles' Brigade</u>
Brigadier General William A. Quarles
4th Louisiana
30th Louisiana
42nd Tennessee
46th & 55th Tennessee
48th Tennessee
49th Tennessee
53rd Tennessee

Cavalry Corps
Kelly's Division
Brigadier General John H. Kelly

Hannon's Brigade
Colonel Moses W. Hannon
53rd Alabama Cavalry
24th Alabama Cavalry Bn.

Allen's Brigade
Brigadier General William Allen
3rd Confederate Cavalry
8th Confederate Cavalry
10th Confederate Cavalry
12th Confederate Cavalry

Humes' Division
Humes' Brigade
Colonel James T. Wheeler
1st Tennessee Cavalry
2nd Tennessee Cavalry
4th Tennessee Cavalry
5th Tennessee Cavalry
9th Tennessee Cavalry

www.ingramcontent.com/pod-product-compliance
Lightning Source LLC
LaVergne TN
LVHW072050060526
838200LV00061B/4705